MARTIN LUTHER KING

IN THE SAME SERIES:

MARTIN
LUTHER
KING

Fighter for Freedom

by Edward Preston

Doubleday & Company, Inc., Garden City, New York

Dedicated to the memory of my mother,
Ralda Bailey Guess—1898–1950

CONTENTS

CHAPTER 1

"Because You Are a Negro"

Martin Luther King, Jr. ran into the kitchen of the big frame house, letting the door slam behind him.

One look at his face told his mother that something was wrong. She hurried across the kitchen to him.

"Martin, have you hurt yourself?"

He shook his head. For a moment he didn't say anything. Then it came out in a rush. "Bill's mother says I can't come to their house any more. Why? Do you know why?"

Mrs. King sighed. "Yes, Martin, I know. Come on into the living room and I will tell you."

They sat down together on the couch and Mrs. King searched for the right words. She knew very well what the trouble was. It was a familiar Southern story. White parents didn't mind their children playing with Negroes when all of them were quite young. But when they started going to school, that attitude changed. Negroes and whites went to separate schools, and white parents saw to it that they were separated as playmates, too.

"Martin," Mrs. King said at last, "it is because you are a Negro and Bill is white. Listen to me, now. I am going to tell you how this all came about, so that you will understand."

She began by telling her son about the tribes in Africa, and of the slave ships that brought the first Negroes from there to America. She told Martin about the slaves in the South, and what their lives had been like. She told him about the Civil War and the Emancipation Proclamation with which Abraham Lincoln set the slaves free.

"But after the Civil War," Mrs. King went on, "the white people didn't want to mix with the Negroes. They knew we were different, and somehow they got the idea that 'different' meant 'not as good.' So we go to different schools, and use different public rest rooms, and sit in the backs of buses or stand so the white people can sit down. It's called segregation."

Martin turned his eyes up to hers. "That isn't fair."

"No," his mother agreed, "it isn't fair. But that's how it is. Some day it will be changed."

"But we aren't slaves any more!"

"No. They say we are free. But we aren't free enough to mix with white people."

Martin sat and thought about it. As far as he could understand, his mother was saying that the United States was divided into two parts—a large white one and a smaller colored one. The colored one was supposed to live quietly and separately on the edge of the white one, disturbing no one, causing no trouble. The colored people—his people—were looked down upon and were not allowed to mix freely in the larger world. That was what segregation meant—an invisible wall between two worlds, no less real because it couldn't be seen.

"But you mustn't think that you're not as good as everyone else."

Martin was only six, but he was a thoughtful and curious boy. He asked his mother, "If I'm as good as anyone, why doesn't Bill's mother want me at their house any more?"

Mrs. King knew that her son's home—his whole life— was a great deal more comfortable than that of most Negroes. Her father, the Reverend Adam Daniel Williams, had been minister of Ebenezer Baptist Church here in Atlanta, Georgia, for 25 years. Martin's own father had been assistant minister and later minister of the same church.

How much, she wondered, could she expect Martin to understand?

Before she could speak, he asked another question. "Why doesn't somebody do something about it?"

"We try," she told him. "Your father, for instance, is a member of the NAACP. That stands for National Association for the Advancement of Colored People. Negroes and some white people, too, belong to it. It has branches all over the country. It fights for equal rights for Negro Americans. It works to get the old laws changed and new, fair laws passed.

"Your father was fighting segregation before you were born," she went on. "He won't ride the buses here in Atlanta because Negroes can sit only in certain seats. And he has worked hard to get Negro teachers better pay. I know Negro teachers aren't paid as well as white teachers, because I was a teacher before I married your father."

She leaned back, smiling. "Did I ever tell you about your father when he was a boy? The first 16 years of his life, your father lived on a farm outside Atlanta. He had nine brothers and sisters, and the whole family worked every day in the fields. They plowed and hoed cotton and thinned and pulled corn and took care of the mules. In the winter, when there wasn't so much to do on the farm, the children went to school for a few months. But it wasn't a very good school—just a one-room shack. And as soon as the weather warmed up they had to stop school and get back to work on the farm.

"Your father could see that his own parents were old before their time, doing what the white boss told them. He saw that colored people did the work and white people took the profit. The colored people lived in shacks and the white people had the money and the fine clothes and the good schools."

"So what did he do about it?" Martin asked.

"He ran away. He told his mother he was leaving because he was going to amount to something. He came here to Atlanta, and he took any kind of job he could to keep going, and he went to school at night. It took him 11 years to graduate from high school. And he didn't stop there. Then he went to Morehouse College. And he began to preach in small churches, too, because by that time he had decided that he wanted to become a minister."

"What happened next?" Martin asked.

"He met a girl—me! We were married on Thanksgiving Day in 1926, and we moved here, to this house, with your grandma and grandpa. After Grandpa died, your father became the minister of Ebenezer Baptist Church."

"And you had three children," Martin put in, getting into the spirit of the story. "Willie Christine, and then me, and then A.D., named after Grandpa."

His mother nodded. "And all that time, Martin, your father was still going to school. He was determined he was going to graduate from college. And he did—16 years after he left the farm to come to Atlanta. He had promised himself he would amount to something, and he kept that promise."

CHAPTER 2

"Why Did I Do It?"

Martin stood looking at all the bright new games and toys on the shelf.

He was eight years old and his mother had taken him shopping in one of the larger downtown department stores in Atlanta.

Suddenly a white women stepped out of the crowd of shoppers. She stopped in front of Martin and slapped his face hard.

"Here's the little nigger that stepped on my foot!" she screamed.

Martin was so surprised and hurt that he couldn't even deny what she said. As quickly as she had appeared, the woman melted away into the crowd.

Biting back tears, Martin stared blankly at the shelf of toys. He would remember for the rest of his life the woman's words and the sting of her slap.

That night, the family sat in the living room together. Martin's father had been told about the woman in the store who had slapped Martin although the boy had done nothing wrong. "It won't always be that way," he said.

Then Martin heard about the time his father had been in the county court house. As he was about to step into an open elevator, a loud voice stopped him.

"Hold on, boy. Your elevator is down the hall."

His father had looked up and seen the elevator operator pointing to a sign near the entrance. "White Only," it read. It was like the signs that Martin saw all over the city. They read "White" or "Colored" or "For Whites Only." They all meant the same thing—Negroes and whites were not to come together.

How, the Reverend King had protested, could a court house, where justice is supposed to be practiced, be segregated? With the aid of lawyers from the NAACP, he fought this practice, and won. The court house elevators became the only public facility in all Atlanta that could be used by both whites and Negroes.

Whenever Reverend King got the chance, he opposed segregation in any form. Once, he and Martin went downtown to buy shoes. They sat down to be fitted like any customers, but the white clerk politely objected.

"I would be glad to wait on you if you would move to those seats in the back," he told Reverend King.

"There's nothing wrong with these seats," Martin's father replied.

The clerk seemed confused, but he had a ready answer that was supposed to settle this sort of situation. "We don't serve colored up here," he explained. "If you want me to serve you, you will have to sit at the back."

"If you don't serve colored in the front, then you don't serve these colored at all," Reverend King told the salesman sharply. He took Martin by the hand and walked out of the store.

Martin was proud to see his father fight back. He made up his mind that when he was grown, he would oppose segregation just as his father was doing.

Another incident at about the same time made it even clearer to Martin that there could be satisfaction in resisting. One day when he and his father were driving downtown, a policeman stopped them.

"Show me your license, boy," he ordered Reverend

King, addressing him by the name Negro men so often were called.

"*He's* a boy," Reverend King replied, pointing to Martin. "I'm a *man.*"

The officer seemed surprised at this reply from a Negro. He handed back the license to Reverend King, muttered some words under his breath, and quickly walked off.

Martin understood that his father would not be treated as a second-class citizen. He was equally influenced by his mother, who was a mild woman with an even temper. His parents' natures were opposite in many ways and something of both was growing in Martin.

To the King family, Sunday was a holy day, a day that was always devoted entirely to church activities. Life was centered around the Ebenezer Baptist Church. The entire family—mother, father, grandmother, Martin and his sister and brother—lived in the rectory, the house that the church provided for its minister.

Through attendance at Sunday school, services and committee meetings, the church became almost a second home to Martin.

For the most part, Martin liked the hours he spent in the church. He especially liked singing. He sang in a clear, high voice, and he sang so well that often his mother was asked to take him to other churches where people wanted to hear him. He wasn't at all nervous about singing. He seemed to belong there at the altar.

As he sat in church one Sunday, listening to a guest minister delivering the sermon, Martin found himself impressed with what the preacher was saying and by the words he chose to express his thoughts.

"Some day," Martin told himself, "I'm going to get some big words like that to use myself."

Martin's life, with the rectory his home and the church his second home, was a comfortable one. But he was a Negro, a fact which he was never fully able to forget. When he went on his afternoon paper route, he saw the shacks that were Negro homes. In their one and two rooms lived families of eight, nine, and ten. Newspapers or tar paper covered the windows to keep out the flies in summer, the cold in winter.

At school, most of his class mates' clothes were ragged. Usually, on Saturdays, he helped his mother pack church baskets of food to take to the poorest families.

Except that he was a Negro, Martin spent these early years in much the same way as any other American boy. He delivered newspapers, sold soft drinks, raked leaves, washed windows and did other odd jobs to earn a little money. When he wasn't working, or attending school, or at choir practice in the church, he played tag or pick-up baseball or roller skated.

Like his friends, Martin much preferred parades, when

they came to town, to either school or church. The year he was 12, the biggest parade of the season was announced as coming on a Sunday. Martin, of course, would not be allowed to see it. Sunday was for church only.

Sunday came. Martin expected to go to the services with his grandmother as usual. His mother had left early and Martin was already dressed before he learned that his grandmother was to be the guest speaker on a women's program at another church. Martin was to go to church alone.

As soon as his grandmother had left the house, Martin slipped out the door and headed for downtown to watch the parade. "What harm can it do?" he thought. "Besides, nobody will ever know."

Martin was small for his age and he wiggled through the crowd on the sidewalk until he reached the front, where he could see the band. Down the street it came, the sun glittering on the gold trimming of the players' fancy uniforms. Martin heard the drums booming out the march time. Then that sound was joined by the blaring trumpets and swinging saxophones.

The crowd was happy, and Martin was having a wonderful time, listening to the bright music.

He was standing there, tapping time with his toes, when he felt a hand on his shoulder.

"Martin! Hey, Martin, listen!"

Martin turned around. It was a friend of his, reaching

out to him through the crowd. "They know I've sneaked off to see the parade," Martin thought. "They've sent for me."

"What's the matter?" he asked.

The boy hesitated. Suddenly he cried, "Your grandmother—she's dead! She had a heart attack—and—and she died!" The boy darted away.

Martin stood still, the parade, the crowd, forgotten.

Sobbing, he pushed his way through the people and ran for home. He knew that, in his grandmother's eyes, running off to see a parade would have been considered a sin. Had she found out? Had he caused his grandmother's death?

When Martin got home, he found the house filled with people. Neighbors and church members had come to comfort the family.

Martin slipped through the front door and into the parlor, hoping nobody had noticed him. On all sides people were weeping and praying aloud. This made him feel more ashamed than ever. Unhappy and frightened, he looked into the faces surrounding him, hoping to find forgiveness in one of them. At last his eyes met his mother's, but he found no comfort there. She turned her head away and wept.

"Why did I do it?" he asked himself. "Why did I run off?"

Upset because he felt so guilty, he fled to the second floor and sat by the back window, looking down at the peaceful garden. He thought about his grandmother and how much he loved her, and he knew his world would never be quite the same place without her. But he also knew, after a while, that her death was not his fault, and that it was foolish to blame himself.

He got up and went slowly down stairs.

Through the sixth grade, Martin went to a segregated school in the neighborhood. In Atlanta, as well as in the rest of the South, Negroes and whites were not allowed to attend the same school. The Negro schools had few books, few desks and often only one or two teachers. As a result, Negro children had much less chance to learn than did white children.

One day, just before Martin was to enter the seventh grade, his father called him into the living room. "Martin," he said, "you are not going back to your school."

For a minute Martin was afraid that he would no longer be going to school at all. Sure, the schools were bad, but it was the only way he could learn anything.

"We are sending you to a different school, a special kind of school set up by Atlanta University."

Martin leaned forward, hopeful.

"This school is segregated, too," his father explained,

"but for a different reason. You see, Martin, this school is run as an experiment to find out if Negro children can learn as much and as rapidly as white students—if their teaching is just as good. And believe me, Martin, this school is a good one."

Martin felt a stir of excitement. Now he would really be able to show what he could do.

At the new school, Martin studied hard and did well. He learned about things that he had never dreamed existed. He learned that history had Negro heroes as well as white ones and that many had given their lives for great causes.

Martin's earlier heroes had been figures from the Bible, but now he began to be interested in men who had more immediate meaning in his life. He learned about the daring Nat Turner and Denmark Vesey, who had led slaves in rising up against their masters. He read about Frederick Douglass, who was born a slave and became a famous statesman.

The stories of these men caught the boy's imagination. They had taken giant steps to aid their own people. It was clear to Martin that more men like that were needed.

After two years, the school shut down through lack of funds. Martin went on to the segregated Booker T. Washington High School, but he was now so well prepared that he skipped grades easily.

Martin had never had any doubts, but at least the point was made. Negroes did do as well as whites if given the same chance. All that remained was to see that they got that chance.

CHAPTER 3

"What Can I Do to Help?"

"All right now, you niggers, get up out of those seats. Can't you see that white folks are standing?"

The driver slowed the bus and turned to glare back over his shoulder.

Here and there, older Negroes began to stand up. Martin and the other students from Atlanta stayed in their seats.

"Listen, you black apes," the driver shouted, "I'm giving you one last chance. Now get on your feet."

Not one of the students made an effort to move.

"Okay, you niggers. I'm getting the police."

The driver headed the bus toward the side of the road.

"Martin!" Miss Bradley called. "I know just how you feel. But remember, this isn't home. We have been sent here as representatives of our school. It's my responsibility to see to it that none of you gets into trouble. Will you do what the man says—for my sake?"

Martin realized the teacher wasn't saying that just to avoid an argument. If the driver called the police, if they were taken to the station to be questioned, Miss Bradley could lose her job. That wouldn't be fair to her. Martin stood up.

"Come on," he whispered. "Do what Miss Bradley says."

One by one, the other students stood up, moving aside to let those who were standing take their seats.

It had all been such a fine experience up to now. Martin had never enjoyed himself more. Not many students of Booker T. Washington High School had ever been on a trip like this. They had been in Valdosta, Georgia, taking part in a high school speech contest.

Miss Grace Bradley, their school's speech teacher, had picked Martin and the other students to represent their school.

To add to the excitement of the trip, Martin had won second prize. When the students gathered at the bus station in Valdosta to return to Atlanta, everyone was in a good mood. The bus was nearly empty and the students sat down in whatever seats looked best.

It was an ordinary scene that changed completely only a few miles farther on. The bus began to stop along the road to pick up passengers. Most of them were white. Soon the seats had all been filled, and some white passengers were left standing.

Nothing was said, and it wasn't until the driver happened to glance in his rear view mirror that the trouble began.

When all the white riders had found seats, the driver continued on his normal route.

Martin said later, "I don't think I have ever been so deeply angry in my life."

By then he knew that violence was possible. His father often received phone calls late at night. When he answered, hoarse voices would shout at him and threaten to burn down the house if he didn't stop pressing for new laws that would be more fair to the Negro.

Those calls, however, had been directed at Martin's father. The incident on the bus had affected *him*, and he found himself repeating his father's angry words: "I am never going to accept this system. I will oppose it until the day I die."

Martin had skipped the ninth grade and gone directly into the tenth at Washington High. In many ways, he was a model student. He was polite to his teachers and he worked hard. More important to Martin right then was the fact that he was able to talk well and could hold his own at a party or in a formal debate on the stage at school.

At dances, Martin was the first out on the floor with the down beat and the last off. Girls found him attractive, with his regular features, and his wardrobe of good suits.

Like most teen agers, Martin had trouble deciding on a career. He was ambitious, but he could find no channel that suited him to carry out his drive. Most of all, even though he was happy in his own small world at Booker T. Washington High School, he longed to move freely in that larger world beyond his horizon.

Although Martin usually showed good sense, he was sometimes impatient, like most boys his age. For instance, he had been waiting months for a certain movie to come to an Atlanta theater. Glancing through the evening newspaper, one afternoon after school, he saw the announcement. The movie had opened in one of the larger, downtown theaters.

Martin decided he couldn't wait for this movie to come to the all-Negro neighborhood theater. As soon as the family dinner was finished, Martin left. It was the first time he had gone out of his neighborhood to see a movie.

It turned out to be one of Martin's saddest experiences. When he got off the bus and bought his ticket at the theater, he found that he couldn't go through the main entrance to find a seat. "Blacks" were expected to go around to a back door and up to the highest balcony, which was called the "peanut gallery."

Martin climbed the dark, narrow stairs, feeling more miserable with each step he took. When he reached the peanut gallery, he saw why it was called that. Peanut shells and candy wrappers littered the floor. The seats were cramped. There was no fan to stir the hot air.

Feeling angry and hurt, Martin dusted off a seat and sat down. But he couldn't keep his mind on the picture.

Years later, he wrote: "I couldn't enjoy the picture . . . The very idea of being separated from the white people did something to my sense of dignity."

More than ever, Martin wanted to take part in the world outside his neighborhood. One day, he asked his parents, "When can I go up North?"

Reverend King looked at his wife. "Martin should go soon. And we do have friends in Hartford, Connecticut." He turned to his son. "How about next week?"

A week later, Martin was on the train to Hartford. As much as he had dreamed about it, he hadn't fully expected what pleasure it was to be able to go anywhere and sit down in any public place without having to enter through a side door.

Now he knew what slaves must have felt when they escaped from their masters and made their way north. Even the air seemed to smell of freedom.

He was still enjoying his new found sense of liberty when he boarded the train for the trip back to Atlanta. Comfortably at ease, he went to the dining car that night—only to find himself shown to a seat behind a curtain, out of view of the others in the car.

Suddenly there it was again, the separation from other people just because he was colored. Once more, segregation had cut him off from the white world. A moment before he had felt like a human being among other human beings. Now that ugly curtain had come down, as if to remind him, "You are black—and you had better remember it next time!"

Martin sat behind the curtain and stared at his dinner, unable to eat a bite. The bitter knowledge of what it meant to be a Negro struck him fully. "And what about those others?" he asked himself. "If this is so crushing to me, what about the farm hands who have to bow down to their white bosses? What about the maids who can't use the toilets in the houses where they work? What about all those who never get a trip North so they can feel free for a little while?"

Finally Martin ate and then slowly went back to his seat. For the rest of the trip he stared solemnly out the window. When the train reached Atlanta, it was a troubled, thoughtful young man who returned to his family.

An important question had become fully formed in his mind: "What can I do to lift up my people?"

CHAPTER 4

Nobody There Was Afraid

"You going to be a preacher like your father?"

It was a question that Martin wasn't ready to answer.

"I don't really know," Martin said slowly, "and that's the truth."

For a long time, his father had made it clear that he hoped Martin would become a minister. The way Martin felt at the moment, church work was far down on his list of careers. He had never openly said so. He had simply kept silent to avoid hurting his father's feelings.

"No need to say anything yet. Let's see what happens in college," he told himself.

It was now the summer after Martin's high school graduation. Directly ahead was his first year at Morehouse College from which his father had graduated. Not yet 16, Martin was one of the youngest students to be admitted.

He had thought seriously about becoming a lawyer to help Negroes come out from behind the curtain that separated them from the rest of the world. Then again, he might follow his mother's wish and become a doctor. Doctors were badly needed in the Negro community.

As for the church, Martin had great respect for his father's personal achievement as a minister, but there were many things about being a minister that did not appeal to him. He didn't like the fact that the church was filled with so many men who could whip up the emotions of their people, but who could do little to help them. Martin felt that there was something wrong in the hand clapping and "amen shouting" that went on in their churches.

Something more was needed, Martin felt sure, something that would speak to the mind as well as to the emotions.

Uncertain about his future, Martin settled on social studies and English as his major subjects at Morehouse College. From social studies, he could learn why people behaved as they did. English would give him a back-ground of language and literature to draw on in his public speaking. Martin now had a lot of "big words" in his vocabulary, and he wanted to learn how to use them as well as possible. Whatever he decided to become later, these courses would give him the foundation he was seeking.

Martin did not make a big splash at Morehouse. He was trying to find his own way and had no desire to attract attention. He sang in the glee club and joined a few organizations, but he did not enter class elections. He was active in the speaking field, however, and won a prize in the annual college contest.

Martin continued to live at home. He was a good student and Benjamin E. Mays, Morehouse President, said later: "I noticed immediately that this boy was old beyond his years. He had a balance and a grasp of life and its problems."

At Morehouse, Martin was encouraged to learn more about other people. He later said of his school: "There was a free atmosphere at Morehouse and it was there that I had my first frank discussion on race. The professors could teach what they wanted with complete freedom. They encouraged us in a search for an answer to race problems, and for the first time in my life, I realized that nobody there was afraid."

Negro colleges were filled with new ideas at that time.

It was just after World War II and there were many discussions of the political future of the Negro. A Southern Negro could go to war and fight for his country, but if he lived and returned home he still couldn't vote in most places. The "home" he had fought to save was most likely a tar paper shack, and the "freedom" he had won was for somebody else.

For himself, he still faced segregation and a lack of jobs and education. It was a bitter time for many Negro soldiers home from the war.

Martin was caught up in these currents of thought. He joined Atlanta's Intercollegiate Council, a group which was made up of both white and Negro students in the colleges around Atlanta. To his great surprise and gratitude, he met white students in this group who had deep sympathy for the Negroes' problems.

Later, Martin admitted that he had been very close to being against all white people before he joined the council. But now he discovered that not all whites looked down on Negroes as "black animals." Many of the younger ones were anxious to be friends.

Like many college students, Martin worked during the summer months. Being the son of Reverend King, he could have had an office job in a Negro-owned business. But that was not for him. He realized that he couldn't learn how badly off some people really were unless he worked side by side with them.

One summer he worked for the Railway Express Company, unloading packages from trucks and trains. It was a back-breaking job but he stuck to it—until the boss called him "nigger."

Another summer he worked in the stock room of a mattress factory. On these jobs, Martin learned a great deal that was valuable to him later.

The thing that impressed him most was that, although Negroes and whites did exactly the same jobs, the Negroes were always paid less. Even so, the white men were not paid enough to maintain a comfortable standard of living.

Martin realized that the poor white Southerner did not have an easy life just because he was white. The sad part of this was that poor whites often expressed their own defeats and disappointments in hate for the Negro.

"There must be some way," Martin thought, "in which all men can have respect for themselves without having to make up for it by hating someone else."

Wasn't the only way through love? But that seemed too simple for him at the time. He had not yet arrived at the idea of non-violence, but the idea of love was planted in his mind. Its growth was helped by Dr. Benjamin E. Mays, President of Morehouse College, and by Dr. George D. Kelsey, professor of religion at the college.

These two men were ministers whose approach to religion was far different from the country "shouting" approach to which Martin objected. They preached a religion that involved the whole person—his mind as well as his feelings. The calm, earnest approach of these two men set Martin to thinking seriously about becoming a minister after all.

It was also about this time, when so many new thoughts were running through Martin's mind, that he read Henry David Thoreau's essay, "On Civil Disobedience." He was struck by the courage of this man, who had refused to pay his poll tax because he believed that a law which forced a person to pay money before he could vote was wrong.

Martin had great respect for the law, but he wondered: "Doesn't a man sin against himself if he obeys laws that are not just—laws that destroy his dignity?"

However, he was well aware of the punishments that awaited the Negro who broke the white man's laws, even though those laws were often unjust.

"If my people could just get over being afraid," Martin thought, "they might lift themselves up from their misery."

But how were they to do that, hemmed in as they were by whites who, for the most part, only wanted to keep them down? What could the Negro really do to help himself? Martin knew what the answer was for many of them: drown their bitterness in drink on Saturday night and moan and pray to the Lord on Sunday morning.

To Martin, this was no answer. But he saw clearly that the church had the same meaning for all Negroes. Whether they were country shouting cotton pickers or college professors, the church was their place of hope.

And what did they find there? Preachers, often uneducated, who could shout and pray with them, but who couldn't lead them out of their trouble.

"Isn't it possible," Martin asked himself, "that a new type of minister—one who is well-trained and who can think as well as preach—is needed to put the Negro on the long road to freedom?"

What his people needed, Martin was certain, was a leader who would teach them not to be afraid. And that leader would have to be, first, a man of God. The mission of leading the Negro to freedom was such a big job that it could only be done with God's help. Martin didn't know whether he could become such a leader or not, but he wanted to try. And the way to begin, he decided, was to become a minister.

When Martin told his father that he had made up his mind to serve in the church, his father was pleased. But he wanted to be sure that Martin had made the right decision. He asked his son to preach a trial sermon.

Martin was only 17, but he already had years of experience before audiences—singing when he was a small child, and making speeches when he was in his teens. At 17 he had developed an easy, friendly manner that drew people to him. On the day of his trial sermon he began to preach in a small section of the church building, but so many people poured in to hear him that the services had to be moved to the church's main hall.

It was a happy day for Martin's father. He had prayed that his son would follow in his foot steps, and now his prayers had been answered.

Martin finished his junior year at Morehouse when he was 18. He could have remained in Atlanta that summer and assisted his father in Ebenezer Baptist Church, but again he chose outside work. Along with his brother A.D. and several of their friends, he went north to Simsbury, Connecticut, to work the tobacco crop.

Once more, Martin enjoyed the freedom from segregation that he had first tasted in Connecticut three years before. When he returned home this time, he was no longer the lonely boy who nursed his hurt behind a curtain in the dining car. Now he was a young man with a mission. That fall he became a minister and elected to be his father's assistant.

Now it was time for the most serious thinking that Martin had ever done. He was beginning his last year of college—more education than all but a handful of Negroes had ever achieved. At 19 he would hold a degree his father hadn't earned until he was more than 30 years old.

What then? If Martin really wanted to be a modern minister, wouldn't he need more—and special—education? Martin knew that he wanted to go to a school of religion, a seminary. Here young men who chose to spend their lives in church work were given special instruction in Bible history and Bible literature.

Martin accepted a scholarship to Crozer Theological Seminary, in Chester, Pennsylvania.

CHAPTER 5

"You Hate Me"

Martin entered Crozer Seminary in the fall of 1948. He was 19. This was the first time he had ever lived away from home. Beyond that, as one of only six Negro students, he was living in a white world.

At Crozer, Martin felt that he should set an example. He knew what kind of picture most white people had of Negroes—always late, laughing, lazy, messy. Martin was going to be the opposite of this image. He thought of himself as on trial.

"I'm afraid I carried out my plan to an extreme," he said of himself afterward. "I kept my room too clean, my shoes were perfectly shined, and my clothes too neatly pressed."

He realized later that he needn't have worried so much. The atmosphere at Crozer was friendly and Martin made friends easily. There was only one exception—and it almost turned into a tragedy.

One of the students, who was from North Carolina, didn't like the idea of having Negroes for class mates. He called them "darkies." This passed without attracting much attention until a student joke brought the Southerner's feelings to a boil.

The students at Crozer were like college boys anywhere else. Among other pranks, they enjoyed staging "room raids." When a student was caught out of his room the others would rush in and tear it up—turning over furniture and scattering clothes and personal things all over the floor. It was meant in fun and was always—or almost always—taken that way.

The young man from North Carolina had taken part in several of these raids on other rooms, but when the joke was played on him he became furious.

Grabbing a pistol he kept hidden in his closet, he raced to Martin's room and beat on the door. Martin opened the door—and found himself facing a loaded gun held by an angry white Southerner.

"I know you did it," the young man shouted at Martin. "You hate me because I don't like niggers. Go on, admit it—and I will kill you right here!"

Martin was surprised, but he answered calmly.

"You must have made a mistake," he said. "What did I do?"

"Don't pull that stuff on me," the white student answered. "I know you were the one who raided my room."

"I haven't been near your room," Martin protested. "Now let's talk this over. . . ."

Other students had gathered around the two and persuaded the angry young man to put down his gun.

The gun incident caused trouble at the seminary and the white student was forced to answer to both the faculty and the student government for what he had done. If Martin had insisted on it, the student would have been expelled—but Martin refused to press charges. The white man felt ashamed and made a public statement saying so.

"Don't keep brooding about it," Martin told him.

"But why should I have threatened to kill you?"

"Perhaps because you know how badly the South has treated the Negro. Here you are reading Christ's words: 'Love thy neighbor.' And you know they are not being followed. You felt guilty, so you acted with violence. Couldn't that be it?"

Before they were graduated, they had become good friends.

Aside from this unusual act of violence, life at Crozer was quiet. Martin had never had trouble with his studies. Now he was in a world of ideas and he was looking for answers to his questions. Where better to seek them than in the thoughts of great men?

This was not just to satisfy personal curiosity. Underneath was a strong desire to discover how best he could apply the teachings of Jesus to help his people. He firmly believed in the words "turn the other cheek" and "love your enemies," but he felt that this was possible only between individuals. He couldn't yet see how it could affect a whole country or lead millions of people out of misery.

Martin read dozens of books during this period, but one that made a lasting impression on him expressed the idea that the teachings of Christ could be applied to life in the world today. Now Martin's thoughts began to take a new direction. For the first time he saw the words of the Bible as a force that could be used to make the world a better place. He felt that the church must play a leading part in helping people to find justice.

During this time, Martin attended a lecture at Fellowship House, one of several sermons given by Mordecai Johnson, then President of Howard University. Johnson had just returned from India, convinced that the idea of non-violence, which Mohandas Gandhi had taught during his life time, could be applied to the race struggle in America.

He described some of the methods Gandhi had used over a 30-year period to achieve his purpose: general strikes and marches—millions of Indians joining, without violence, in protests against the British Government.

Gandhi, like Martin, had been influenced by Thoreau's writings, which he had read in a South African jail cell. Martin was impressed by the courage of this man who, without violence, had gained so much.

After the lecture, Martin bought every book he could find on the life and work of Mohandas K. Gandhi. His own hopes and ideas were beginning to take shape now. He felt he could see a way to channel the teachings of Christ, Thoreau, and Gandhi into a method of working that would help his people. He saw that the principles of all three men flowed into each other, and he imagined their coming together in a mighty stream so strong it would wash away the Negroes' troubles and fears.

Now the idea of non-violence meant something practical to Martin, not just a dream. It could be used—*he* could use it—to help the Negroes of America achieve freedom.

Years later, when Martin led the bus protest in Montgomery, Alabama, it was Gandhi's words that he spoke to convince those who refused to ride. "Rivers of blood may have to flow before we gain our freedom," he said, "but it must be *our* blood."

Another time he gave his people strength by repeating these words of Gandhi's: ". . . violence may be called body-force. If I do not obey the law and accept the punishment . . . I use soul-force."

Soul-force, non-violence, love—these were the ideas that Martin Luther King, Jr. took with him when he was graduated from Crozer Theological Seminary in 1951. He knew that when the right time came he would put them into practice without fear.

CHAPTER 6

A New World

"What now?"

Martin was standing on the thick green of the seminary lawn after graduation ceremonies.

He had ended his studies at the head of his class and had been voted class president. On top of this, he had won a $1200 grant allowing him to continue his studies at any university he chose.

"Are you ready now to be a minister?" Martin's father had asked him.

Martin had answered, "There's so much left I want to know more about. I'd like to take graduate studies at Boston University."

"You are perfectly ready now to become the minister of a church."

"I know, Father. Crozer has taught me a great deal. But I need to know more about myself."

That fall, Martin drove up to Boston in the green Chevrolet his parents had given him as a graduation present. Boston had been the seat of revolutionary ideas since the beginnings of the United States. In Boston's Cambridge area were Harvard, one of the great U.S. universities, and Radcliffe College for Women. Henry David Thoreau, the author of "On Civil Disobedience," had attended Harvard. So had Ralph Waldo Emerson, author of the famous essay, "On Self Reliance," and other men whose ideas had influenced the thoughts and acts of men everywhere.

Martin enrolled for courses at Harvard and discovered, to his delight, that it was still the seat of new ideas.

He took an apartment with an old friend of his from Morehouse, Philip Lenud. Lenud was now a student at Tufts University, which was also near Boston. It wasn't long before their apartment on Massachusetts Avenue was a meeting place for students of all races and religions.

Martin's life in Boston was active, and he felt it was complete. But that was before he met Coretta Scott.

Coretta was studying to become a concert singer at the New England Conservatory of Music. She was two years older than Martin and had struggled to get an education.

Her father, Obie Scott, was an independent Negro business man in Heiberger, Alabama. The Scott family had owned their land since the Civil War. Mr. Scott was in direct competition with local white business men, and they were bitter about this. When Coretta was a child, her father's life was often threatened.

Coretta was head of her class in the first six grades at Crossroads School, a segregated grammar school near her home. For many Negro children, that was all the education available to them. Coretta was lucky to be able to go on. Lincoln School, run by church missions with both Negro and white teachers, was located in Marion, a town near where Coretta lived.

Attending this school brought the young girl into touch with a whole new world. When Coretta graduated from Lincoln she was given a race relations money grant to go to Antioch College in Yellow Springs, Ohio. At this college, students went to classes for six months and then worked for six months. During the "work" months, Coretta had many different jobs—in a restaurant, in a settlement house, and once in a library in New York.

Coretta majored in education. She planned at the time to become a teacher, but her first love was music. The head of the Department of Music at Antioch urged her to apply for a grant to the New England Conservatory.

Coretta waited several weeks for a reply to her application, but there was no word. Finally, she left for Boston anyhow. She had made up her mind.

"I have worked before," she told herself, "and I can work again and save money so that I can study music."

Then, at the last minute, the grant did come through. But it covered only her studies and didn't include room and board. After Coretta paid for her courses, she had nothing left for food. She went hungry for several days, eating only peanut butter and fruit.

Then she found a part time job, and later she received help from the State of Alabama. The State aided Negro college students to study elsewhere—an arrangement that avoided their being admitted to colleges in Alabama.

Circumstances improved for Coretta, but she still wasn't happy. She had been away from home for a long time, and now she was alone in a big city. With her studies at the music school and her part time job, she didn't have much chance to meet people.

But when a friend from Atlanta told her that there was a young minister, also from Atlanta, who wanted to meet her, Coretta wasn't very interested. She remembered the ministers from her childhood—narrow minded men who were not very well trained. She said firmly, "No, thank you."

Her friend insisted that this Martin Luther King was very different from the picture Coretta had in her mind. Finally, Coretta gave in and said that Martin could call her. He did—and he talked so long on the phone that Coretta became curious to meet him. She agreed to a date.

When Martin drove up to meet Coretta, her first thought was: "He's too short!"

Martin was only five feet, seven inches. However, Coretta found him as interesting as he had sounded on the phone, and she soon forgot about his height. At the end of the date, Martin told her: "You have all the qualities that I expect to find in the girl I'd like to have for a wife."

Coretta was so surprised that she couldn't reply. But when he asked if he could see her again, she quickly said yes. Soon they were spending as much time together as their studies would allow.

Coretta realized that Martin was an exceptional man, but she had no thought of marriage. She had the future carefully planned: she would complete her musical studies and begin her career before she married. But within a few months, Martin began a serious campaign to change her time table. And Coretta discovered that her plans were no longer so important, after all.

On June 18, 1953, Martin and Coretta were married in the garden of her home at Heiberger, Alabama. Martin's father performed the ceremony.

Returning to Boston, the young couple took an apartment near the music school. Coretta finished her studies and Martin finished his courses. He had now earned his degree, Doctor of Philosophy, which gave him the right to call himself "Doctor" King.

When the new Dr. King began looking around for a position, he received more good offers than he knew what to do with. Two churches in the North and two in the South asked him to be their minister. He also had offers from three colleges: One was to teach, one was to work in administration, and the third was for the position of dean—the head of one of the schools in the college.

"I feel myself pulled in all different directions at once," he told Coretta. "You know, I've always wanted to be some kind of teacher. But then, the pulpit is so rewarding in so many ways. It's hard to decide what to do."

Also, he pointed out, they had to decide whether to remain in the freedom of the North or return to the segregated South. Coretta was especially worried about bringing up children in the South and having them experience the same problems that she and Martin had. Too, she wanted to continue studying music and have a career of her own. This would be much easier to do in a Northern city.

They talked and prayed for several days. Then one night after supper, Martin said, "You know, I've been thinking of home."

"So have I," Coretta answered.

"I think we have a duty to go back," Martin continued. "We could have a much nicer life up here, but in a way it would be selfish to stay. Somehow I don't think we have the right to take an easy way out for ourselves. There are still all those people down there who may never find any way out unless we help them."

"You are right, Martin," Coretta agreed quietly. "We should go back—at least for a few years."

They knew the troubles they might run into. They had often spoken of them. But they didn't speak of them now.

"I think I will write the Dexter Avenue Church," Martin said at last. "I think that's the best for now. Maybe I can teach later."

One of the church offers he had received was from the Dexter Avenue Baptist Church in Montgomery, Alabama. He wrote that he was interested in accepting the "call" to become their minister. This particular church appealed to Martin because many of its members were on the faculty of Alabama State College and were people with whom he had common interests.

He preached his trial sermon at Dexter in May 1954. The congregation accepted him—even though one lady did remark that the 25-year-old minister "looks lost up there without his mother."

On September 1, 1954, the Kings moved into the house provided by the church.

Every student of American history remembers that Montgomery was the capital of the Confederacy. It was here, on the steps of the government building, that Jefferson Davis became President of the Confederate States of America on February 18, 1861. Nearly a hundred years later the building was as beautiful as ever.

Across the square from it was the Dexter Avenue Baptist Church. No one thought then that history was about to be made again in that old square—an entirely different kind of history.

The Montgomery of 1954 had changed little since 1861. It was still a sleepy Southern town. Of course, it had grown in the meantime. Now it had a population of 130,000, of which 80,000 were white people and 50,-000 were Negroes. It was a large market for lumber and cattle, but there was no heavy industry. The only jobs for Negroes other than working as servants or for Negro employers were at Maxwell and Gunther Air Force bases.

Strangely enough, the bases were completely integrated,

though outside their gates it was a different story. Montgomery was completely segregated. The United States Supreme Court decision banning school segregation was handed down in May 1954, but the white people of the city didn't seem to think that it applied to Montgomery. The city gave the impression that it was still the seat of the Confederacy.

The Montgomery city buses helped carry out that impression and kept the two races separated. White passengers sat in the front and Negroes in the back only. If the seats were filled, Negroes had to stand up and let the white people sit.

Voting in Montgomery was also an almost completely white privilege. Of the Negroes who were of an age to vote, only 2,000 were registered. Many Negroes had been kept from the polls by threats of violence, or through fear of losing their jobs.

This was the situation that faced Martin Luther King, Jr. in September 1954. He wanted to join professional organizations, but he found that they were all segregated. The membership of the NAACP was 100 percent Negro. The *only* meeting place for the two races was the Alabama Council on Human Relations, which Dr. King joined.

His main interest at that time, however, was in his church. He was glad that the membership in the church included many educated people, but he felt that it should take in the whole community. To accomplish this end, he set up new church committees: for social service, for political action and for religious education. There was also a committee to raise money to help high school graduates attend college and one to encourage young artists.

These committees proved more successful than Dr. King had expected. He had been afraid that the congregation would not want to take on so many new projects all at once, but they quickly offered their services. The new minister also urged all church members to register to vote. Both the number of church members and the number of people who registered to vote increased rapidly.

After Dr. King had begun the new programs at Dexter Church, he moved out into the community. There he found the situation quite different. The Negro community was not only separated from the white—it was also divided within itself.

It did not have a single leader but several, and each had his own followers. Often, instead of getting together behind a big issue that affected the whole community, they would spend their energies in competition with each other.

The NAACP was involved mainly in legal actions. Less than a year after joining it, Dr. King was elected to the executive committee. He was able, through this group, to become familiar with the courts and court actions. Also, his membership in the Alabama Council on Human Relations opened up a line of communication between Negroes and whites. Two white ministers on this council, the Reverends Thomas P. Thrasher and Robert Graetz, were of great support in the struggle that came later.

There were several other social and political groups, but they couldn't get together on any one program of action to improve the condition of life for Negroes in the city. The Citizens Coordinating Committee was formed early in 1955 to try to bring these groups together with a common goal. But it failed to achieve its purpose and broke up after a few months.

Fear and divisions within their ranks had prevented the Negroes of Montgomery from making much headway against segregation. They needed, everyone agreed, an *act* to cause them to unite.

On the first of December, the act was provided by Mrs. Rosa Parks. This quiet lady brought the Negro community together in a way it had never known before.

CHAPTER 7

Three Days to Get Ready

Mrs. Rosa Parks might have seemed an odd person to make history, but as Martin Luther King, Jr. said later, she was actually perfect for the role. She was a lady with the courage to defend her human rights—in this case, her right to a seat on a bus.

On that first day of December 1955, Mrs. Parks was on her way home from work in a downtown department store. She had done some shopping after work and she was tired. On the bus home she was seated in the Negro section, behind the white section.

When more white passengers got on, the driver turned around as usual and said, "Stand up back there so these people can have seats."

Three Negroes got up at once. Mrs. Parks remained seated.

"I'm asking you again to get up back there," the driver said, a little louder.

Mrs. Parks did not get up. She acted as if she hadn't heard him at all.

"You won't get up?" he shouted. "All right, I'm going to fix you."

He stopped the bus, got off and called the police.

A few minutes later a policeman boarded the bus, with the driver behind him. The driver pointed out Mrs. Parks, still sitting quietly in her seat.

The officer didn't ask Mrs. Parks to give up her seat. He just said: "You are under arrest."

Mrs. Parks was not unknown to people of influence in the Negro community. She had once been secretary to E. D. Nixon, when he was president of the local branch of the NAACP. As soon as Mr. Nixon heard of Mrs. Parks' arrest, he went to sign the bond for her release.

This led to some press statements that Mrs. Parks had been "planted" by the NAACP in order to get a test court case. But the woman's own words were simply: "I don't really know why I wouldn't move. There was no plan. My feet hurt."

She might have paid her fine and the incident would have been closed, without even getting into the local papers. Several such cases had gone that way before. But the arrest of Mrs. Parks touched off sparks that had been gathering for a long time.

Many other Negro passengers had been insulted by white drivers. Nor was it unusual for a bus driver to wave a loaded gun and threaten Negroes who got "out of their place."

If a Negro entered the front door, he was told to get off and board the bus from the rear door. Often, before he could get there, the bus would drive off. These incidents had piled up over the years, and with the arrest of Mrs. Parks, things came to a head.

There was anger and talk of protest from the very beginning. Through E. D. Nixon, word quickly got around to the Women's Political Council. They suggested that Negroes boycott the buses—refuse to ride in them at all. Mr. Nixon agreed to lead the boycott, and got on the telephone to begin rounding up support. One of his calls was to Martin Luther King.

Without even stopping to say "Hello," Mr. Nixon described what had happened. He finished by saying: "We have taken this type of thing too long already."

Dr. King agreed immediately that some form of protest was necessary and that he would support it. He then telephoned several other prominent ministers to arrange a meeting that night of Negro church and city leaders, offering the Dexter Avenue Baptist Church as a meeting place.

The news of Mrs. Parks' arrest spread quickly through the Negro community. By two o'clock that afternoon one group was already distributing printed notices announcing the bus boycott. This was less than 24 hours after Mrs. Parks had refused to give up her bus seat to a white man.

It was a warm winter evening and the turn out was larger than Dr. King had dared hope for. Over 40 people from every level of Negro life showed up. There were doctors and lawyers and teachers. There were also business men, postmen and labor leaders. For once, the ministers forgot their differences and united behind the protest.

As soon as the meeting opened, the chairman, Reverend L. Roy Bennett, president of the Interdenominational Ministerial Alliance, told everyone the reason why they all were there. Then he proposed that the Negroes should boycott the buses on Monday, December 5. "This is no time to talk; it is time to act," he concluded.

Others present agreed with him about the boycott, but they had questions and suggestions. They began to call to the chairman to let them speak. When he consented to yield the floor, practical questions were asked. How long would the boycott last? How would word be spread to the entire Negro community? How would people get to work and back home again?

Finally, they were all agreed that the boycott would go into effect on the following Monday, December 5, and that a mass meeting would be held that night to determine the success of the boycott and whether it should continue. A statement was then prepared to be printed and distributed the next day, Saturday.

It read:

Don't ride the buses to work, to town, to school, or any place Monday, December 5.

Another Negro woman has been arrested and put in jail because she refused to give up her bus seat.

Don't ride the buses to work, to town, to school, or anywhere on Monday. If you work, take a cab, or share a ride, or walk.

Come to a mass meeting, Monday at 7:00 P.M., at the Holt Street Baptist Church for further instruction.

Yet the big question remained to be answered: How would the 17,500 Negroes who rode the buses every day get to their jobs in the morning and back home at night?

It was fortunate that Montgomery had 210 taxis from 18 different Negro-owned companies. Usually, there was severe competition among these companies, but each of them agreed to transport people for the same price as the bus fare—ten cents a piece.

At midnight, the meeting broke up. Everyone felt something important had been accomplished.

By nine o'clock Saturday morning, 7,000 notices announcing the boycott had been printed. Within an hour or two, dozens of students and women gathered to distribute them. In this, they received help from an unexpected quarter.

A Negro maid who couldn't read had been given one of the early notices on Friday afternoon. Wanting to know what was printed on it, she had asked her white employer what it said. Her employer was so angered by what she read that she called the local newspaper, the *Montgomery Advertiser*. The *Advertiser* felt obliged to let its white readers know what the Negroes were up to and printed the story on the front page of the paper Saturday morning.

This was a happy accident, as the article served to tell the entire Negro population of the proposed boycott. Therefore, when it was announced from the pulpits of Negro churches on Sunday morning, the people were already informed and aroused.

That Sunday afternoon Dr. King sat in deep thought. Coretta was busy with their new baby, Yolanda, who had been born scarcely two weeks earlier, and he was alone in his study. He thought about the serious consequences of the boycotts led by the White Citizens' Councils. These Councils had been set up for the sole purpose of fighting the U. S. Supreme Court's 1954 ruling against school segregation. Their methods had included economic boycotts against merchants who didn't agree with them, as well as threats and violence.

"I wonder if we are not trying to fight evil with evil," Dr. King said to himself. But as he thought it over from all angles, he decided that the bus boycott was truly an honest protest against the unfair treatment of the Negro. The White Citizens' Councils had used boycotts to deprive the Negro of his rights under the law. But the purpose of the bus boycott was to give the rights of human dignity to everyone. Dr. King came to this conclusion: "Our concern would not be to put the bus company out of business, but to put justice in business."

He recalled what Henry Thoreau had written in "On Civil Disobedience." Thoreau had advised men to disobey laws that were not just. It was not, however, a matter of simply disobeying such laws, King reflected. It was really a matter of the Negroes lending their help to injustice or refusing to do so.

He felt that if the Negroes continued to ride the segregated buses they would be approving the system and encouraging it to continue. The protest was the only moral course to take.

His doubts stilled, a weary Dr. King prepared for bed. The last three days had been busy ones, and he needed sleep before the big day tomorrow.

The time for action had come.

CHAPTER 8

"Get Tough"

By 5:30 the next morning, Martin and Coretta King were already up, dressed and waiting for the first bus to roll by.

At six, Dr. King was in the kitchen when his wife called, "Martin, come quickly!" She pointed to a bus in front and shouted, "Look, it's empty!"

The bus line that ran by their house usually carried more Negro passengers then any line in Montgomery.

A second bus was also empty, and so was a third! The boycott was really on.

Dr. King raced to his car and drove all over town to have a look at the other buses. They, too, were empty. All day long the buses rolled, but Negroes, except for a very few, did not ride them. They rode in cabs, in private cars; some rode mules and some even traveled in old-fashioned buggies. Many walked long distances, starting early to get to work on time.

At 9:30 that morning Mrs. Parks was tried, found guilty, and fined ten dollars, plus court costs of four dollars. She appealed the sentence. Mrs. Parks' conviction gave the movement extra energy on its very first day. The people now had someone to look up to.

At three that afternoon Reverend Bennett called the ministers and leaders together to plan the mass meeting for that night. The leaders suggested that an organization be formed to make decisions and long range plans. After several names were considered, it was decided to call the new organization the Montgomery Improvement Association (MIA).

An election of officers was then called and Martin Luther King, Jr. was elected president.

This took him by surprise, as he had not sought office in local groups. Shortly before this he had refused to run for president of the local NAACP branch.

Thinking it over later, King remarked that he thought

65

he was elected because he was so new to Montgomery that he had not had time to become connected with any single group. This may have been part of the reason, but it also seems true to suppose that the other members of the new MIA had already recognized him as a leader.

The men at this meeting were of different opinions on other matters. Some suggested that since the one-day boycott had been so successful in showing the power the Negroes were suddenly able to muster, it should be called off. It had made its point, they said. Some were afraid that if it continued it would die out in a few days and the white people would only laugh it off. This was a strong argument, but it was agreed to wait until that evening and let the people decide.

The leaders' meeting finished so late that the mass meeting was only a half hour away when Dr. King arrived home to prepare his speech. He was used to spending 15 hours a week on his Sunday sermon. Now he had only 20 minutes before he had to leave for the Holt Street Church.

"How can I think of just the right thing to say in 20 minutes?" he asked himself. He paced the floor, trying to think. He looked at his watch. Five minutes had passed already.

At the thought of the effect that his speech could have on other people, he felt strong misgivings.

"I have to arouse them to action," he told himself.

"But then what? Some of those people who will be there are bitter, really bitter, and if they get aroused in the wrong way, I don't know what they might do."

Somehow, he decided, he would have to get them to keep their anger within moderate Christian bounds. He didn't know exactly how he would accomplish this, but he knew that that was the general message he had to get across. And he would have to do it without a written speech or even notes.

When he got within five blocks of the Holt Street Church, Dr. King was stopped by a huge traffic jam. He parked and walked the rest of the way. Several thousand people were waiting outside—the seats inside had been filled since five o'clock. The speakers had to push their way through to the platform.

The meeting began with thousands of voices raised in the old hymn, "Onward Christian Soldiers." Then, with TV cameras directed on him, Dr. King rose to speak. First, he reviewed the many abuses Negro passengers had endured on the buses.

"But there comes a time," he went on, "that people get tired . . . tired of being segregated; tired of being kicked about. . . . We have nothing else to do but to protest."

His words were met with applause from the audience. He reminded them of the violent methods of the Ku Klux Klan. The audience stirred at the mention of this hated and feared group. At one time or another, each of them had seen Klansmen. Masked by their peaked hoods and white robes, they rode into Negro neighborhoods, burned crosses on lawns, and threatened the people. Sometimes they would drag a Negro from his home and hang him—without fear of being caught and charged by white law officers.

"But in our protest there will be no cross burnings," Dr. King assured the audience. "No white person will be taken from his home by a hooded Negro mob and murdered. Our method will be to persuade. Once again we must hear the words of Jesus echoing across the centuries: *Love your enemies, bless them that curse you and pray for them that despitefully use you.* . . . In spite of the bad treatment that we have met with, we must not become bitter and end up by hating our white brothers. As Booker T. Washington said, 'Let no man pull you so low as to make you hate him.' "

He was stopped by cheers and had to wait several minutes before he could finish. In closing, he said, "If you will protest with courage, and yet with dignity and Christian love, when the history books are written in the future, those who write them will have to pause and say, 'There lived a great people—a black people—who put new meaning and dignity into the veins of civilization.' This is our challenge and our great responsibility."

Now came the time for the rules and plans, which

were read by Reverend Ralph Abernathy, minister of Montgomery's First Baptist Church. Mainly, they asked the Negroes not to ride the buses until (1) they were guaranteed polite treatment from the drivers, (2) passengers were seated on a first-come, first-served basis—with Negroes seated from the back and whites seated from the front, and (3) Negro drivers were hired for routes through Negro neighborhoods.

Happy shouts rang out and the plans were quickly adopted. The decision to continue the boycott was made and the people themselves had made it.

In these first demands, complete integration was not suggested—at that time, such a thing was beyond the wildest hopes of even the Negro leaders.

The boycott continued and within three days the leaders of the city government agreed to meet. It was a hopeful sign, but the meeting came to nothing. The chief of police did not oppose the plan, but the mayor of Montgomery did. Even more strongly opposed was the lawyer for the bus lines, who insisted that the rules would be against the city's segregation laws.

"If we granted the Negroes these demands," he said, "they would go about boasting of a victory over the white people, and this we will not stand for."

The city agreed to guarantee polite treatment and that was all. It would not agree to any change in seating arrangement nor to hire Negro drivers, even though it admitted that 75 percent of its riders were Negroes.

Before the meeting broke up, Police Chief Clyde Sellers mentioned that there was a law requiring taxi drivers to charge no less than 45 cents a fare. Dr. King took this as a hint that the dime taxi service was about to be halted, and he began preparing for it. He quickly called an old friend who had led a similar boycott in Baton Rouge, Louisiana, by setting up a car pool. This friend supplied him with a complete description of operating details.

At a mass meeting that same night, Dr. King asked for volunteers to form a car pool. A hundred and fifty people offered their cars at once. Later, the pool was to swell to over 300 cars. Wealthy ladies drove workers in their Cadillacs, and several white men from the Army bases around Montgomery joined the pool in their off-duty hours.

Just as Dr. King had thought, the police chief cracked down on the taxis less than 24 hours later. But by that time the car pool was already in full swing.

Next, a net work of 48 "leave" and 42 "pick-up" stations was set up. Most of the stations were in Negro churches, which opened their doors and provided heat against the cold winter mornings. The whole operation ran so well that even the White Citizens' Council admitted that it was like a military operation.

The Christmas season was approaching, but the gay spirit of the boycotters had nothing to do with the calendar. Even though a ride was found for almost everyone who requested it, some preferred to walk as an act of pride. One old lady said, "I'm not walking for myself. I'm walking for my children and my grand children."

Very shortly after the boycott got under way it hit the front pages of newspapers around the world. Letters poured in from all corners of the globe, many of them containing checks. They came from places as far apart as Singapore and Pennsylvania, and from men on board ships at sea. A Swiss woman sent $500.

These letters were almost too much for the small MIA group to handle. Regular offices and a full staff were badly needed. Dr. King was soon worn out from the vast number of telephone calls he was receiving. People called from five in the morning until late at night.

To handle all the problems that the boycott was causing, the MIA added ten people to its office staff and looked for a place to house them. As soon as they settled down somewhere, the whites who opposed them would begin driving them out.

They moved from their first office, in a church center, because the whites on the church board said they would not support the center if the MIA was allowed to remain. Their next home, a club, was told it would lose its license if they were not put out. At last they were given permanent quarters in the new building of the Brick-layers' Union. The union owned the building and all of its officers and most of its members were Negroes.

The costs of continuing the boycott were mounting, but so was the amount of money that people were sending in. Churches, associations of ministers, labor groups, social clubs sent funds from all over America. Branches of the NAACP gave financial as well as moral and legal support.

The fund swelled to $250,000, which not only served to keep the movement going, but helped to prop up flagging spirits. The people knew that they were surrounded by many who were against them, but it was encouraging to realize that beyond that immediate ring of hate there were many who supported them, both black and white.

It was a white woman, Miss Juliette Morgan, who wrote the *Montgomery Advertiser* that the bus protest could be compared to the movement led by Gandhi in India. For daring to express such thoughts in public, she was cut off by the white community.

After the first meeting with Montgomery city officials, the MIA discovered that the bus line was owned by the National City Bus Lines, Inc. of Chicago. A list of their demands was sent by telegram to the president, along with a request that the company send a representative to Montgomery to meet with them. The president replied

Dr. King poses with Rosa Parks at an SCLC dinner held in her honor at a desegregated Birmingham hotel on August 10, 1965. Dr. Ralph Abernathy is seated at left. Mrs. Parks' refusal to give up her bus seat to a white man led to the Montgomery bus boycott in 1955. UPI

Nine "Freedom Riders" defy the "White Only" sign in a Trailways Bus Station waiting room in Montgomery, Alabama, in 1961. UPI

Tense moment before Negro First Baptist Church in Montgomery, May 21, 1961. Martial law was declared by Alabama Governor Patterson after a white mob tried to storm the church, skirmishing with Federal marshals. The meeting was to hear Rev. Martin Luther King, Jr. UPI

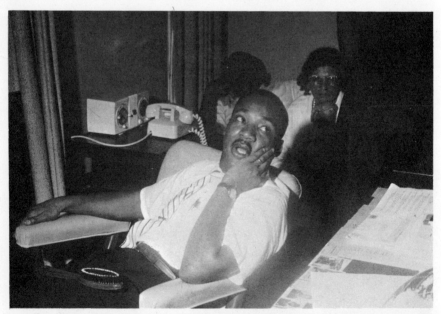

Rev. King, Rev. Abernathy and other civil rights leaders marooned in the office of the Negro First Baptist Church while violence rages outside. Later that night they were escorted home by National Guardsmen. UPI

President Kennedy and UN official Adlai Stevenson meet with Negro leaders at the White House in December, 1962. Left to right: unidentified man; Roy Wilkins, Executive Secretary of NAACP; Dr. King, Adlai Stevenson and President Kennedy. UPI

Civil disobedience "Prayer March" on Birmingham during 1963 campaign. Dr. Abernathy (left) and Dr. King (right) were both arrested, along with more than fifty others. UPI

Negro demonstrators, many of them children, mowed down by high-powered waterhoses wielded by Birmingham firemen. UPI

"Prayer Pilgrimage" in Birmingham is broken up as police dog sinks his teeth into the arm of an unidentified Negro demonstrator. UPI

Baseball star Jackie Robinson stands before the bombed home of Rev. A. D. King in Birmingham. The bombings followed new desegregation rulings. Robinson and ex-heavyweight champion Floyd Patterson visited Mrs. A. D. King. UPI

Leaders of the 1963 March on Washington link arms and march along Constitution Avenue toward the Lincoln Memorial where Rev. King gave his famous "I Have A Dream" speech. Roy Wilkins, Executive Secretary of NAACP, is at the far right. Dr. King is in the center. UPI

Police officers inspect damage to an auto before the shattered windows of the Sixteenth Street Baptist Church in Birmingham following a dynamite blast. Four little girls were killed and numerous others injured after a bomb was thrown from a car during Sunday school. The bombers were never caught. UPI

Rev. King conducts a funeral service for the four girls killed by the bomb blast. He told the overflowing crowd: "The spilled blood of these young girls may cause the white South to come to terms with its conscience." UPI

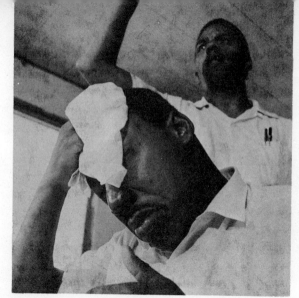

June 17, 1964, a hot day in St. Augustine, Florida. In asking for Federal protection for demonstrators, Dr. King called St. Augustine "the most lawless community I have ever seen." UPI

Dr. King and Dr. Abernathy in a jail cell in St. Augustine after their arrest on "trespass" charges. They had conducted a sit-in at a segregated motel restaurant. UPI

Dr. King receiving an honorary Doctor of Laws degree from Yale President Dr. Kingman Brewer. After the ceremony he returned to the campaign in St. Augustine. UPI

Rev. King and Rev. Abernathy in an audience with Pope Paul VI at the Vatican in September, 1964. The pontiff expressed sympathy with the demonstrators in America and asked Dr. King for copies of his latest books. UPI

Dr. King receiving the Nobel Peace Prize from Gunnar Jahn, chairman of the Nobel Prize Committee, in Oslo, Norway, December 10, 1964. Dr. King was honored for his non-violent leadership of the American movement for civil rights. UPI

Sheriff Jim Clark blocks the doorway of the Dallas County Courthouse in Selma to keep civil rights leaders from entering. Left to right: Rev. Andrew Young, Rev. Martin Luther King and Rev. Ralph Abernathy. UPI

Dr. King addressing a rally during a voter registration drive in Selma, Alabama, February, 1965. When Dr. King was thrown in jail in Selma he said "There are more Negroes in jail with me than there are on the voters' polls in Selma." UPI

March, 1965, Marion, Alabama. Rev. King conducts a funeral service for
Jimmie Lee Jackson, another victim of racial violence. Jackson, 26, was
shot during a demonstration. UPI

On the road. Rev. King and Rev. Abernathy change socks during the first
phase of the Selma-to-Montgomery march. UPI

A happy moment for Dr. and Mrs. King as they rejoined the Selma-to-Montgomery march. Thousands of Americans joined the last leg of the march on March 3, 1965. For Dr. King it was a triumphant return to Montgomery. UPI

Dr. King leads the last leg of the triumphal procession to Montgomery. In the front row are John Lewis of SNCC (2nd left), Rev. Abernathy (3rd left), UN official Ralph Bunche (5th left), Rev. King, Mrs. King, Rev. Fred Shuttlesworth, Rev. Hosea Williams of SCLC, carrying a little girl. UPI

Civil rights leaders in the forefront of an anti-war demonstration in New York, April 15, 1967. Dr. King urged a halt in the bombing. Left to right: Dr. Benjamin Spock, Dr. King, Msgr. Charles Rice, and Cleveland Robinson, chairman of the Negro American Labor Council. UPI

April 8, 1968, Memphis, Tennessee. Mrs. Martin Luther King, Jr., surrounded by National Guardsmen as she prepared to lead a memorial
march in honor of her husband who was slain in Memphis four days
before. An estimated 10,000 persons, including Harry Belafonte (wearing
sun glasses), joined in the tribute. UPI

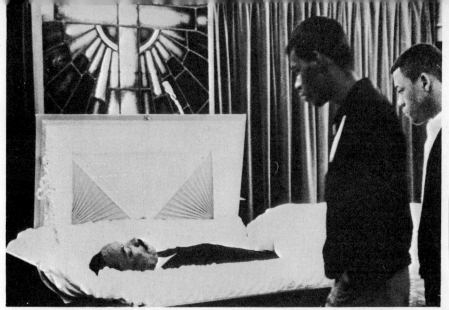

Two teen-agers view the body of Dr. King, lying in state before his funeral. Thousands of Americans lined up to file past his casket. UPI

April, 9, 1968. Mrs. Martin Luther King, Jr., widow of the slain civil rights leader, holds her youngest daughter, five-year-old Bernice, during the funeral service at the Ebenezer Baptist Church in Atlanta. UPI

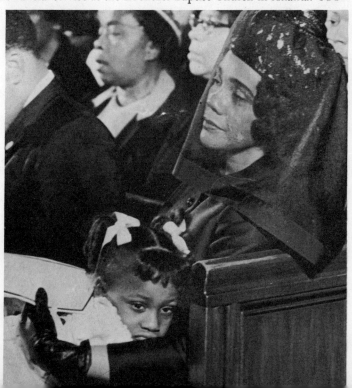

A farm wagon drawn by two mules bears the body of Dr. King from Ebenezer Baptist Church to a memorial service at Morehouse College. UPI

that he would send someone down in the next few days.

The representative arrived, but the MIA only found out about it through white friends a few days later. He met with the city officials but did not contact the "rebels." Another meeting was called by the mayor for December 17. The man from the bus company was there, but it soon became obvious that the city had already convinced him that right was on their side. He opposed the boycott.

This second meeting also included the white ministers of the First Baptist and St. James Methodist Churches. Reverend Frazier of the Methodist church defended segregation and advised the ministers in the MIA to lead the souls of their followers to God and away from social problems.

This meeting also ended with no solution, though the mayor did appoint a committee to meet with representatives from the bus company and the MIA. At first he tried to stack the committee with eight whites and only two Negroes, but when the Negroes objected, he backed down and agreed to appoint an equal number of both races. Another meeting was called for Monday, December 19.

It got off to a bad start when the secretary of the local White Citizens' Council, who was not a member of the mayor's committee, rose to speak. Dr. King at once challenged his right to do so because of his record of speeches against the Negroes. The white members then attacked Dr. King, accusing him of standing in the way of an agreement.

This was actually the first of many attempts to divide the Negro leaders. However, Reverend Ralph Abernathy came to Dr. King's defense and informed the committee that King spoke for the entire Negro group, not just for himself.

The third meeting also produced no results. The white Baptist minister who had headed the mayor's committee promised to call another meeting, but he never did.

Since the white citizens had failed to force the Negroes to end the boycott or give up some of their demands, they began to use other means. Negro employees were told that their leaders were using them for their own profit. A false story was spread that Dr. King had bought a Cadillac for himself and a Buick station wagon for his wife. White leaders went to Negro ministers and attempted to stir up trouble among them by telling them that "these new out-of-town preachers have grabbed the power that really belongs to you."

Dr. King was so upset by these stories that he offered to resign as president of the MIA. But the other officers would not hear of this.

Christmas came and went, the New Year arrived, and still the boycott continued. The Negro and white communities seemed farther apart than ever.

There were no further official meetings, but one group of white business men, calling themselves the Men of Montgomery, met on two different occasions with MIA officials to try to reach a settlement. These men were not anxious to speed integration, but they could see that the boycott was already having a bad effect on business. After all, they reasoned, Negroes were customers, too. These men seemed to be sincere in their efforts, but the city leaders refused to discuss the matter with them.

On Sunday, January 22, the city announced to their former passengers, and to the world press, that they had worked out a "settlement" with a group of three prominent Negro ministers. The terms of the so-called settlement were these: (1) a guarantee that Negroes would be treated politely; (2) a white section at the front, a Negro section at the rear with a first-come, first-served middle section; (3) special, all-Negro buses during rush hours.

It was fortunate that an out-of-town news man noticed this story when it first came over the wire service on Saturday and called Dr. King to find out if it were true. King expressed his surprise. He had heard nothing of a settlement and couldn't imagine who the three "prominent" ministers could be, as all the prominent Negro ministers in Montgomery were members of the MIA. He asked the news man to try to get the names of these three.

The city refused to release their names but did give their churches. The news man turned these over to Dr. King, who began telephoning ministers all over Montgomery until he found the three. As it turned out, they were neither prominent nor members of the MIA. They had simply been invited by telephone to discuss a new insurance plan for the city. Each of them insisted that he had had nothing to do with any "settlement" and each later publicly denied the city's report.

Meanwhile, Dr. King had called a special meeting of the officers of the MIA. By the time they had found out all about the false story, it was almost midnight. Something had to be done to warn the Negroes that the article they would read in the next morning's paper was false.

Dr. King glanced around at the other leaders in the room. "Gentlemen," he said, "there's only one thing to do. We have to go straight to the people, wherever we can find them."

The others agreed and reached for their coats and hats. Negroes in night clubs and dance halls that Saturday night were surprised to see Dr. King and other ministers enter.

"Why, Reverend," one man laughed, "we expect to see you in church but never in here."

The ministers gave their message and went on. To spread the word, they went to movie theaters, street corners, pool rooms—anywhere that Negroes might be gathered. This took them far into the night, but they were so successful that the buses were empty as usual the next morning.

The city's white leaders realized that they had once again faced a force that they could neither defeat nor understand. Three of those men—Mayor W. A. Gayle, Police Chief Clyde Sellers and City Commissioner Frank A. Parks—declared that they had joined the White Citizens' Council. The mayor announced a new policy he was sure would work: "Get tough!"

CHAPTER 9

"Your House Has Been Bombed"

Mayor Gayle's "Get Tough" policy got started quickly. Drivers in the car pool were stopped and forced to show their licenses and insurance papers. Riders waiting at pick-up points were warned that they could be arrested for hitch hiking. The city was out to break the movement. The Negroes countered by buying 15 new station wagons and adding them to the pool.

Shortly afterward, Martin Luther King was arrested "for going 30 miles in a 25-mile zone." The police took him along back roads, and he feared that he was going to be turned over to a white mob. Actually, the police were trying to avoid being seen with their prisoner, but word of the arrest soon spread.

Within two hours a huge crowd had gathered in front of the jail. To avoid a disturbance, the police allowed Reverend Abernathy to pay a cash bond for the prisoner's release.

Several days later, Martin Luther King returned to court and was found guilty of the traffic charge. He paid a ten-dollar fine and although he felt he had not been treated fairly, he was glad that no serious trouble had come of his arrest.

During the next few days the city was quiet, but for the King family the nights were becoming times of terror. They began to receive threatening telephone calls—calls that were increasingly violent.

"Sometimes," Martin Luther King told his friend Reverend Abernathy, "I don't know that I will live another day. Every time I leave the house I wonder if it is the last time I will see Coretta and the baby."

"You mustn't worry," his friend said. "God will protect you."

The threatening calls continued. Near the end of January, Dr. King picked up the phone and heard a low voice growl: "Listen, nigger, we've taken all we want from you. Before next week, you will be sorry you ever came to Montgomery."

This latest call left Martin Luther King more discouraged and frightened than he had ever been. He felt helpless, unable to go on. Alone at the kitchen table, he prayed to God to give him strength to continue.

What happened seemed a miracle to him. He felt that a divine presence had entered him, and he heard an inner voice saying: "Stand up for truth and God will be at your side forever." He arose with a new strength and faith.

A few nights later, Martin Luther King's faith was put to a terrible test. He was at a mass meeting at the First Baptist Church, standing up on the platform, when he noticed a man give a whispered message to Reverend Abernathy. Abernathy ran downstairs and came back a minute later looking worried. Several other people ran in and out.

Dr. King realized that something had happened and that it affected him. But what? He went over to Abernathy and said, "Tell me, Ralph, what's wrong?"

Reverend Abernathy hesitated for a moment. Then he said, "Martin, your house has been bombed."

Martin Luther King caught his breath. "Coretta and the baby—are they all right?"

Abernathy admitted that no one was sure, but people were checking.

Calmly calling the meeting to order, Dr. King told the crowd that he had to leave, and why. He urged all those present not to get excited or resort to violence.

"Let us keep moving," he advised them, "with the faith that what we are doing is right, and with the even greater faith that God is with us in the struggle."

When he reached home, he rushed into the house, pushing through the hundreds of angry Negroes gathered in front. He burst into the bedroom to find that Coretta and "Yoki"—his nickname for little Yolanda—were safe. Coretta told him that she and a woman friend who was with her had heard something land on the front porch. They had run to the back of the house, reaching it just before the bomb exploded.

A deeply relieved Dr. King went out to face the crowd. The police were already there, trying, without success, to clear the street. The crowd was in no mood for the police. Many of the men were armed. One wrong word— and violence would break out.

Martin Luther King spoke to the crowd: "If you have weapons, take them home," he told them. "We cannot solve this problem through violence. Remember the words of Jesus: 'He who lives by the sword will perish by the sword.'

"We must love our white brothers, no matter what they do to us. . . . We must meet hate with love. Remember, if I am stopped, this movement will not stop, because God is with the movement. Go home with this glowing faith."

The mayor and the police chief had arrived, and the chief tried to speak. After many hisses and boos from the crowd, he was able to say that a reward was being offered for information leading to the capture of the persons who had committed this crime. Slowly, the crowd broke up, and the people returned to their homes.

A leader of Dr. King's church turned to Mayor Gayle and said, "You may express your regrets, but you must face the fact that your public statements created the atmosphere for this bombing. This is the result of your 'Get Tough' policy." The mayor did not reply.

After the crowd and the police had left, Dr. King, his wife, and baby went to a friend's house to spend the night. Later, lying awake in bed, he began to think about the bombing incident in all its horror. It seemed that his faith and strength were crumbling. "How could anybody do such a terrible thing?" he asked himself. "Coretta and Yoki might have been killed!"

Suddenly, he felt himself filled with hate, not only for the men who had thrown the bomb, but for the white city leaders and the police, too. "They are just as evil," he told himself.

He lay there for a long while before he calmed down. Finally he convinced himself, as he had convinced the crowd, that they must all meet hate with love. He found himself saying out loud, "You must not allow yourself to become bitter."

Two nights later, a stick of dynamite landed in front of E. D. Nixon's home. Again, no one was hurt. A large crowd soon gathered before the house, but they kept themselves under control. It was another victory for non-violence.

Meanwhile, lawyers had found an old state law which said that it was illegal for two or more persons to block the operation of a legitimate business. The Montgomery County Grand Jury debated for a week, decided that the boycott was not legal and issued orders for the arrest of a hundred people. The list included all the leaders of the movement.

Martin Luther King was at Fisk University in Nashville, giving a series of lectures, when he heard that the arrests were scheduled to begin. He decided to return and be arrested with the others. But first he flew to Atlanta to see his parents and his wife and daughter, who were visiting them.

Several friends gathered at the senior King's home and urged Martin not to return. He listened, then answered, "I would be a coward to stay away. I would rather be in jail ten years than desert my people now." Two days later he returned to Montgomery.

When Dr. King went to the jail to turn himself in, he found a cheerful atmosphere. Those on the list had joyfully presented themselves for arrest. News men from all over America, and from England, France and India, were there to cover the story.

The trial lasted four days, and 28 witnesses were called. Among them was Mrs. Stella Brooks, who described how her husband had been shot by a policeman when he asked for his dime back on a filled-up bus. Later, he had died of his wounds.

Mrs. Martha Walker told of the time when she was leading her blind husband from a bus. The driver slammed the door shut on her husband's leg, and he was dragged down the block.

Mrs. Georgia Gilmore said to Judge Carter: "When they count the money, they do not know Negro money from white money."

Dr. King was found guilty and sentenced to 386 days at hard labor on the county prison farm, or $500 and court costs. The case was immediately appealed, and several friends came forward to sign his bond.

When they came out of the court room, the Kings were surrounded by TV and newspaper camera men. Dr. King had become a hero to the Negroes of Montgomery with his first arrest. This second arrest and conviction brought him international attention.

The leaders of the boycott had realized all along that the issue went beyond the Montgomery bus struggle. They had asked the United States District Court to end bus segregation because it violated the Fourteenth Amendment of the United States Constitution.

Three federal judges, after debating the issue for nearly three weeks, came to a decision on June 4, 1956. They declared, by a two-to-one vote, that the bus segregation laws of Alabama were unconstitutional. The city did not accept this decision and appealed it to the United States Supreme Court.

But the decision did not mean that troubles were over for the Kings. The telephone calls and letters had stopped after their home had been bombed, but now they began again. These hate calls were mixed with calls from well wishers, both white and Negro. However, the hate calls increased to such an extent that the Kings had to get a telephone number that was not listed.

There were other problems as well. White insurance companies stopped the insurance on the station wagons. However, Lloyd's of London agreed to sell the MIA insurance for the cars.

The long, dusty summer months went by and faded into autumn, and the Negroes of Montgomery still walked or rode in the car pool. At last, in a final attempt to destroy the boycott, the city asked the courts on October 30 to stop the pool completely. They claimed that it was not a legal transportation system.

Negroes then requested that the city not be allowed to interfere with the pool. It was a bitter disappointment when their request was denied by the federal district judge.

The hearing on the city request was set for Tuesday, November 13, before Judge Carter, the same judge who had convicted Martin Luther King and others a few months before for operating a business that was not legal.

The Negroes felt sure that they would lose. Dr. King went to the meeting that night with grave doubts. If the car pool was stopped, what would they do? He didn't have the heart to ask all the people to walk. In an effort to raise their spirits, he said, "This may well be the darkest hour just before dawn."

The issues in court the next morning boiled down to this question: "Is a car pool a private business operating without a license or is it a non-profit 'share-a-ride' plan that needs no license?"

Before the question could be answered there was a sudden stir in the back of the room. Dr. King turned to a friend and said, "Something is wrong."

A moment later a news man came up to him and thrust a piece of paper into his hand. Trembling, he read the words: "The United States Supreme Court today agreed with a decision of a special three-judge U. S. District Court in declaring Alabama's state and local laws requiring segregation on buses against the Constitution."

Dr. King told his lawyer, then almost ran to the back

86

of the court to break the good news to Mrs. King, Reverend Abernathy and E. D. Nixon.

Word of the decision spread through the room like electric sparks. The feelings of the Negroes were expressed by an unknown man in the crowd who said: "God has spoken from Washington, D.C."

The Negroes of Montgomery had won their battle.

A mass meeting was called for the next night, November 14. Eight thousand people gathered in two churches to hear the Bible read, to sing songs of thanksgiving and to celebrate. One old lady told a news man: "My feets is tired but my soul is at rest."

Later that night the hooded figures of the Ku Klux Klan rode through the streets of the Negro sections. Usually when they appeared, Negroes turned out the lights and stayed quietly in their houses. This time they were not afraid. People who were sitting and talking on their front proches kept on sitting and talking. Some of them waved to the passing Klansmen. One little boy called inside to his sister, "Hey, Sis, come out and watch the parade."

The Klan members were so confused by this reaction that they soon rode off into the night, without burning a cross or threatening anybody.

Several days passed and the court order had not arrived. The car pool had been stopped. Just as expected, Judge Carter granted the city the right to halt the car pool—but his move had little effect. A "share-a-ride" plan was worked out to take the place of the car pool. The city officials, realizing that they were beaten, did not interfere.

During the waiting period, training in the policy of non-violence continued. Dr. King reminded the people: "We must not take this as a victory over the white man, but as a victory for justice and democracy."

The bus integration order finally reached Montgomery on December 20. On December 21, 1956, 381 days after the boycott began, a strange scene took place in that Alabama city.

At 5:55 A.M., Martin Luther King, Reverend Abernathy, E. D. Nixon, and Reverend Glenn Smiley, a white Southern minister, walked from the King home to the bus stop in front. They were followed by TV and newspaper camera men and reporters from every continent.

The white driver smiled and greeted the passengers politely as they boarded. When Dr. King put his dime in the box, the driver said: "I believe you are Reverend King, aren't you?"

"Yes, I am," Dr. King replied.

"We are glad to have you this morning," the driver said.

Martin Luther King thanked him and took his seat. Montgomery's first integrated bus rolled down the street.

CHAPTER 10

"I Can't Stop Now"

Negro bus riders stuck to their pledge to shun violence, the first few days of integration passed in peace. However, in spite of all efforts to prepare the Negro community for this social change, no effort was made to prepare the white community. City officials warned that blood would be shed—and certain people took this as a signal and an order.

Within a week after the buses were integrated, the terror began. A Negro woman was shot in the leg. Buses were fired upon—which gave the city an excuse to stop service after five o'clock. The Ku Klux Klan paraded again and again.

Hand bills appeared suddenly on bus seats and tacked up on fences, urging Negroes to "quit Reverend King before it is too late." These warnings claimed to be from other Negroes who complained, "We get shot while he rides. He is getting us in more trouble every day. Wake up! Run him out of town!"

As strong as these arguments seemed to be, the Negroes of Montgomery assumed that they were issued by whites to frighten them, and paid no attention. They continued quietly about their business.

Then on January 9, 1957, Martin Luther King and Reverend Abernathy went to Atlanta for a meeting of Negro leaders. The meeting was to start the next day, but they had come early to prepare for it and were staying at the home of Dr. King's parents. They had gone to bed early, hoping for a good night's sleep.

At two in the morning the silence of the sleeping household was broken by the ring of the telephone. Dr. King answered it. It was Mrs. Abernathy, calling from Montgomery. A few minutes later, Abernathy turned from the phone, a pained expression on his face. "My home has been bombed," he said. "And there were several other bombs set off in the city."

Dr. King asked about his own wife and daughter.

"They're safe, thank God," Abernathy told him.

Before either of them could say another word, the phone rang a second time. It was Mrs. Abernathy again to say that her husband's church had also been bombed. In despair, the two men prayed for help and strength.

It was now three in the morning. In the next four hours, the phone rang 15 times—each time with news of another horror. The home of Reverend Robert Graetz, a white minister, had also been hit. Three Negro churches had been completely destroyed.

The two men also received the alarming news that crowds of Negroes had gathered at each of the bombing sites. They were controlling their anger, but how long would it be before they struck back?

Dr. King and Dr. Abernathy returned to Montgomery at once. As they expected, they found the Negro community deep in despair. All the city buses had been halted and it seemed as if every gain won in the boycott had been lost.

But then the white people of Montgomery began to speak out against such acts. Several white ministers went on the radio to say that the bombings were wrong. The Men of Montgomery, an organization of leading business men, also protested the violence.

These words from whites brought temporary quiet to Montgomery—but it was shattered early in the morning of

January 28. Again, bombs were thrown at Negro businesses and homes.

The night before, Martin Luther King had gone to stay with friends on the other side of town. Once again, he experienced the dreadful sensation of hearing the telephone ring like a fire alarm in the middle of the night. The call was to tell him that a bomb, made of 12 sticks of dynamite, had been found smoking on the front porch of his home.

He thanked God that Coretta and the baby had left for a visit to Atlanta the day before. He and his host hurried into their clothes and raced across town. On the way they saw other scenes of disaster where bombs had exploded, but they were relieved to learn that no one had been injured.

When they arrived at the King home they found a huge crowd gathered in front. The slightest encouragement would have turned these people into a rioting mob. Dr. King managed to prevent this by repeating the words he had said so many times before: "We must not return violence under any condition. I know this is difficult advice to follow. . . . But this is the way of Christ; it is the way of the Cross."

As it was Sunday, he asked the people to go home and prepare for church. Slowly, a few at a time, they drifted away.

After this latest display of violence, the white people

of Montgomery rose in great numbers to protest. At last the city was forced to act. Rewards were offered for information about the bombings. On January 31, seven men were arrested. The wave of terror ended, and the integrated buses resumed their full schedules.

The effects of the victory in Montgomery were wide spread. It became a sign of hope to Negroes throughout the country. Strength and dignity were discovered again, and a new pride was born.

The Negroes of Montgomery won admiration for their calm conduct, and it did not come only from people in the North or in foreign countries. Admiration and respect also came from Montgomery's white citizens, many of whom had at first been completely opposed to integration of the buses.

If the long campaign of non-violence changed the face of the South, it also changed the life of Martin Luther King, Jr. At the beginning of the boycott he was unknown, except in a small circle. At the end of it, his name was known in every country on earth. He was only 28 years old, but he was already being compared to Gandhi. One magazine called him "a kind of modern Moses . . ."

Honors began to pour in from all sides. He received many requests to speak and could have earned thousands of dollars a month lecturing. A number of Northern churches and universities offered him positions.

King weighed all these offers and remained the head

of the Dexter Avenue Baptist Church in Montgomery. He was a preacher first, he decided, and then a leader.

At that point, when his fame had reached its first peak, Martin Luther King could easily have left his people behind. But, although he was the one who had gained international recognition, he considered the thousands who had walked through snow and rain, and who had refused to return violence with violence, to be the real heroes. He looked upon himself as their leader but not as their superior.

Montgomery was only the beginning of a long struggle to bring Negroes into the main stream of American life. The movement would go on, and Martin Luther King, Jr. had already decided that he would go on with it.

In January 1957, he had met in Atlanta with 60 Negro leaders, most of them ministers. They had formed the Southern Christian Leadership Conference, SCLC. He was elected president of this body and remained in that office for the rest of his life.

The purpose of the SCLC was to hold on to the gains made by the Negro through the Montgomery campaign and to continue the spirit of non-violence in making greater gains. Other Negro communities in the South felt the need to "do something about our situation" and looked to the group for help. The later bus boycotts in Atlanta, Tallahassee, and other cities could be traced back to the successful Montgomery boycott.

One of the SCLC's first appeals was to the White House. President Eisenhower was asked to come South and lend the authority of his office to help integration. In answer, they were told the President had no time.

After being encouraged by recent Supreme Court decisions, the leaders of the movement had expected more. But during the bus boycott, the President had been quoted as saying: "I don't believe you can change the hearts of men with laws."

Dr. King had thought many times about the President's statement. And just as many times he had told himself that he did not agree. "Maybe you can't change men's hearts by laws," he reasoned, "but you can certainly help control how they act and behave."

How, then, did you get new laws passed that would accomplish that? First, he decided, you had to elect the right leaders to office, and one way to do that was to have more Negroes register to vote. The more Martin Luther King thought about it, the more convinced he became that the Negro would never make any great strides as long as he was denied his right to vote.

Not long afterward, Dr. King and other leaders planned a prayer journey to Washington. It was scheduled for May 17. The prayer journey turned into a national event. Almost 30,000 Negro and white Americans came together before the Lincoln Memorial in the nation's capital.

The other speakers had all had experience in arousing the emotions of audiences, but it was Martin Luther King, Jr. who brought the crowd to its feet.

"Give us the vote and we will no longer plead," he said. "We will write the proper laws on the books. Give us the vote and we will fill the government with good men. Give us the vote and we will get . . . judges who love mercy. Give us the vote and we will quietly carry out the May 17, 1954 decision of the Supreme Court. . . . Give us the vote and we will change the bad deeds of the mobs into the planned good deeds of peaceful citizens."

At the end of King's address, the audience burst into cheers. This was his first speech before a national audience, and he came out at the end of it as the most important Negro leader in America.

In August of 1957 Congress passed a civil rights bill, but it was so weak that it did little to break the pattern of segregation. Martin Luther King accepted the bill for what it was. He continued to make dozens of speeches around the country, insisting that the federal government enter the civil rights struggle. He also repeated his request for a White House conference.

This request was finally granted on June 23, 1958. President Eisenhower agreed to meet with Dr. King, A. Philip Randolph, a prominent civil rights and labor leader, Roy Wilkins of the NAACP, and Lester Granger, then executive director of the Urban League. Randolph spoke for the leaders and read nine points that were proposed to the President.

The Chief Executive was asked to stand squarely behind civil rights laws. He was urged to give the Justice Department power to protect Negroes in their attempts to register to vote. He was also requested to direct the Justice Department to act to halt the bombings and burning of churches in the South. Finally, the President was asked to oppose the use of federal money for projects such as schools and hospitals that practiced segregation.

Martin Luther King continued to bring the situation of the American Negro to the attention of the American public at large. He was one of the most popular speakers of the century, traveling 780,000 miles in 1958 to give 208 speeches.

In September 1958, two incidents occurred which reflected the public's attitude toward Dr. King. On September 3, he was arrested in Montgomery for "loitering" and thrown in jail. He was released on bond a few hours later but decided to serve his 14-day sentence. However, when he presented himself to serve the term, the police chief, Clyde Sellers, paid the fine out of his own pocket and would not allow him to go to jail. This was the same police officer who had taken part in an all-out war against the bus boycott only two years before.

The next incident occurred a little over two weeks

later. On September 17, Dr. King's first book, *Stride Toward Freedom*, was published. It was his own account of the Montgomery story. On September 19, he was signing copies of the book in Blumstein's, a Harlem department store, when a Negro woman stepped from the crowd and asked, "Are you Mr. King?"

When he replied, "Yes, I am," she cursed and plunged a letter opener into his chest.

The people in the store turned into a screaming mob, and one woman almost ended King's life instantly by trying to pull the weapon out of his chest. The letter opener's sharp tip had reached the main vein of his body, and if he had so much as sneezed he would have drowned in his own blood.

A team of doctors at Harlem Hospital spent three hours performing an operation to remove the weapon. Mrs. Izola Curry, the woman who stabbed him, was put in an institution for the insane.

While he was recovering, "get well" messages and flowers piled up in Dr. King's room. Averell Harriman, then Governor of New York, made a personal visit. King himself expressed surprise that there was "so much business" about the attempt on his life, but it was clear that America and the world cared what happened to him.

After he was fully recovered, Dr. King, along with Mrs. King and his close friend, Lawrence D. Reddick, made a trip to India. For years he had dreamed of paying tribute to the work of Gandhi and the land he had freed through his teaching of non-violence. He told Prime Minister Nehru: "To others I may go to see the sights, but to India I come as a pilgrim."

He returned to America with new belief in love as a moving force and in non-violence as a method. However, the wave of bombings that exploded all through the South in 1959 made it obvious that many white Southerners did not agree with him.

Rumbles had also begun to be heard among the Negroes themselves. The black nationalist movement, led by Elijah Muhammed, which for years had been small and relatively weak, now gathered strength. Its followers wanted to establish a separate Negro state and had little patience with the ideas of love and non-violence. Partly due to the success of the Montgomery bus boycott led by Dr. King, and partly due to the rise of other new leaders from among their people, the Negro in America was on the march.

The struggle for equality covered a larger canvas than it had three years before. This challenging, highly charged situation forced Dr. King to ask himself whether he should remain in the church or move out into the wider field of civil rights—or try to do both.

He had been swamped with high paying offers for several years, but had not accepted any of them. "After all," he had said to Coretta, "I owe something to

Montgomery, and to the Dexter Church. After our success with the boycott, I can't just walk off and leave all these people."

"I agree with you entirely," Coretta had told him. "Montgomery has been good to us, in spite of everything."

However, Martin Luther King knew that if he wanted to extend his activities he would have to go to a larger city to do so.

For several reasons, he felt drawn to Atlanta. In the first place it was his home town. Also, there was Ebenezer Baptist Church, and his father's offer to share the pulpit with him.

Finally, all the reasons in favor of going came together in his mind, and he decided to make the move to Atlanta. There, he could remain in the ministry and at the same time play a leading part in the battles that lay ahead.

In December 1959, Dr. King announced to the members of the Dexter Avenue Baptist Church that he was resigning. He summed up by saying: "I can't stop now. History has thrust something upon me which I cannot turn away."

When he finished, the people linked hands and sang "Blest Be the Tie that Binds," an old hymn always sung at times of parting.

Martin Luther King, Jr. broke down and wept.

CHAPTER 11

Sit-In to Freedom

When Martin Luther King, Jr. returned to Atlanta, Reverend Abernathy went with him. Dr. Abernathy held various positions in SCLC and became one of the leaders of the city's Negroes. Dr. King once described him as "my closest associate and most trusted friend. We prayed together and made important decisions together. His ready good humor lighted many tense moments."

Shortly after he arrived in Atlanta, Dr. King announced: "The proper time has come for a bold advance. . . . We must not let the present opportunity pass."

However, before he could propose a full program, a new and independent development occurred. On February 1, 1959, four Negro students sat down at a lunch counter in Greensboro, North Carolina, and refused to move until they were either served or arrested. From this small beginning, the sit-in movement spread all through the South.

Sit-ins were held in department stores, restaurants, markets, theaters, libraries—any place that barred Negroes or segregated them. The sit-ins grew to include stand-ins, kneel-ins and mass marches, all conducted without violence.

Dr. King recognized at once that this new movement, led mostly by students, had been inspired by the Montgomery success, and he offered his personal help.

Before he was able to take part, however, he was arrested on a warrant from the State of Alabama and charged with making out a false state income tax return. The case broke down when a state tax agent admitted under cross examination that he had found no evidence of a false return.

An all-white jury freed Dr. King, but this case affected him deeply. He had never before been accused of cheating.

In April 1960, two hundred college students who had

been active in the new demonstrations met for a conference. Martin Luther King was the principal speaker. He told the students that they would need "some kind of continuing organization." As a result, the Student Non-violent Coordinating Committee (SNCC) was formed. SNCC followed the policy of non-violence for about five years but then abandoned it.

In May, Martin Luther King was arrested for driving without a Georgia driver's license. When the case was heard in September, he was given a 12-month suspended sentence, meaning one which he did not have to serve, provided he stayed out of trouble with the law during that time. This did not seem important at the moment.

A month later, he and 51 others were arrested during a sit-in at Rich's department store in Atlanta. The others were released, but Dr. King was held for breaking his sentence. Then he was sentenced by the court to four months at hard labor.

By the time he reached the prison, telegrams from around the world were pouring into the Atlanta mayor's office. Meanwhile, the Department of Justice prepared a statement. President Eisenhower was requested to issue it. The statement attacked the jailing of Dr. King as being "unjust." But President Eisenhower did not issue the statement, and Vice-President Nixon said that he would "have no comment."

The 1960 campaign for President was then at its

height. The Democratic candidate, Senator John F. Kennedy, called Mrs. King to express his concern and pledge his support. The Senator's brother, Robert Kennedy, called the judge "to inquire as to whether the Reverend Martin Luther King had a right, under the Constitution, to bail."

King was released at once and returned to Atlanta in a rented airplane. Eisenhower remarked later that "a couple of phone calls" had put Kennedy in the White House.

After John Kennedy had become President, Martin Luther King still felt the federal government was moving too slowly and said: "The President has proposed a ten-year plan to put a man on the moon. We do not yet have a plan to put a Negro in the state government of Alabama."

However, there was progress. The Justice Department began many law suits to gain voting rights for Negroes and to integrate schools.

The sit-in demonstrations, backed up by suits, continued without much violence. However, trouble from Southern whites broke out once again when the Freedom Rides began in May 1961.

These bus rides, taken by Negroes and whites together, had a definite purpose—to dramatize the fact that transportation was still segregated in the South, even though such segregation was forbidden by Federal law.

The first Freedom Bus, with 13 students, left Washington on May 4. Nothing happened until it reached Anniston, Alabama—but there, a furious mob of whites was waiting. The Freedom Riders barely escaped being burned up or blown up, but this did not stop them from boarding another bus headed for Birmingham. When they arrived there, they were attacked and beaten by another mob.

A second group was attacked in Montgomery on May 20. The violence got so out of hand that Attorney General Robert F. Kennedy ordered 400 U.S. marshals to the city to keep order.

A mass meeting was called for the next night in the First Baptist Church. Martin Luther King was the main speaker. With a thousand people attending, it was very much like the mass meetings of the bus boycotters five years before. One big difference was the second crowd that had gathered in front of the church. They were white—and they were out for blood.

The church filled up while the white mob controlled the area around it. A group of marshals and a few city policemen stood between the two. Suddenly the mob went out of control and began throwing bottles and stones. The marshals answered with tear gas.

While fighting continued outside, the crowd inside the church joined hands and sang "We Shall Overcome," which had become the battle song of the Freedom Movement.

The National Guard then moved in and scattered the mob. Martin Luther King and the other speakers were rescued and taken to their homes by the Guard in the early hours of the morning.

The Freedom Rides grew in number after that, with the ranks of the riders swelled by white church men of all faiths. They rode the buses with the students and went to jail with them when arrested by Southern police.

The Freedom Rides accomplished their purpose. The Interstate Commerce Commission banned all segregated transportation between the states and also banned segregation in the waiting rooms, toilets, and restaurants of bus and train stations.

Much had been achieved in just a few years. Part of a dream had become reality. From one boycott in one town, the movement had grown so large that the entire Government of the United States was involved.

What should be the next goal? It was important that there be no slowing down now. If that happened, everything that had been accomplished could be wiped out. Martin Luther King returned to Atlanta and began planning a new project. The operation was worked out in secret. Few staff members were told any of the details.

The plan was known only as "Project C."

CHAPTER 12

Letter from a Jail

Project C was simple.

There was one city in the deep South that stood rock fast in refusing to grant the Negro any civil rights.

If Martin Luther King's peaceful protest plan could be brought to Birmingham, Alabama, and made to work, there would be no limit to what could be accomplished.

It would not be easy.

The major problem was Commissioner of Public Safety

Eugene "Bull" Connor. Connor had long prided himself on his ability to "keep the Negroes in their place."

The city had closed ranks behind Connor. When the Reverend Fred Shuttlesworth and his group, The Alabama Christian Movement for Human Rights, won a court suit to open the town parks to Negroes, Birmingham ordered the parks closed altogether.

Plan C was set to begin April 3, 1963. At first there were only a few sit-ins and a small number of arrests. In the meantime, mass meetings were being held every night in Negro churches. Bail money had already been obtained. Most of it had come from the North. The singer Harry Belafonte had been particularly successful in raising funds. The NAACP had virtually bankrupted itself by posting about $250,000 in bail for Freedom Riders and demonstrators. Little or none of it was ever recovered.

More workers came forward daily. Each was required to turn in any personal weapons he might have and promise not to use violence under any circumstances.

Project C was slow in starting. It was not immediately accepted by the Negro community. In fact, there were complaints that the movement was being led by people from the outside, who came in to stir up trouble that the permanent Negro residents would have to pay for when the others left.

April 6 had been marked for the first march on City

Hall. It was not intended to be a mass demonstration and it wasn't, but it turned out to have a different kind of effect from the one the leaders had expected.

When the marchers made their way through the downtown streets they were not bothered. Policemen milled around them but did not interfere with their progress. There were many Negroes on the sidewalk, watching the march.

Then suddenly, three blocks from City Hall, a group of police blocked the street. The police captain barked to the marchers: "I order you to halt!"

When they continued to march forward, the police began making arrests. The police were ready for resistance, but they were not prepared for what happened next. Instead of resisting, the marchers burst out singing! They kept on singing freedom songs while they were herded into police vans.

The Negroes who were watching could hardly believe their eyes and ears. With the voices of the marchers filling the street with song, they felt proud, and they began to cheer.

Forty-two were arrested from that first march on City Hall—not many compared to the mass arrests that began a few days later. But something else had been accomplished. Now that it had its own heroes, the Negro community began to unite.

After that incident, the demonstrations increased every

day. Kneel-ins were held at segregated white churches. Read-ins were held in libraries. A campaign to register Negro voters was opened. There was also a boycott of downtown stores.

On April 10, the city officials obtained a court order banning demonstrations entirely. Dr. King felt that the order must not be obeyed, even though he knew that he and hundreds of others would be arrested.

Staff members begged him not to join the marchers, for a new problem had come up. It was not possible to continue putting up bail money for those who were jailed. This was a great blow to the campaign, and Dr. King was urged to avoid arrest so that he could raise the needed money. However, he felt that he could not ask other people to expose themselves to arrest and not do so himself.

Dr. King and Reverend Abernathy led the march the next day protesting the court order, and were quickly arrested when they reached the downtown area. Dr. King was not allowed to see anyone.

Mrs. King had given birth to a daughter, Bernice, just two weeks before. For two days she heard nothing from or about her husband.

On Easter Sunday she was so upset that she tried to reach President Kennedy, who was spending the holiday in Palm Beach, Florida. She was put through to Press Secretary Pierre Salinger, who called Attorney General

Robert Kennedy in Washington. The Attorney General called Mrs. King to say that he would check on the situation. He called again a few hours later to report that Dr. King was safe.

The next day the President called to tell Mrs. King that he had arranged to have Dr. King speak to her. He also gave her the comforting news that he had sent the FBI into Birmingham.

In a dark jail cell, unable to talk with anyone, unable even to see daylight, Dr. King borrowed paper from a guard and wrote his famous "Letter from a Birmingham Jail." It was addressed to his fellow ministers.

"I am in Birmingham because injustice is here," he wrote. "There are two types of laws: There are *just* laws and there are *unjust* laws."

In reply to charges that the peaceful protest movement was not legal, he wrote: ". . . We can never forget that everything Hitler did in Germany was 'legal' and everything the Hungarians fighting for freedom did in Hungary was 'illegal.'

"I have no fear about the outcome of our struggle in Birmingham," he continued, "even if our motives are at present misunderstood. We will reach the goal of freedom in Birmingham and all over the nation, because the goal of America is freedom."

This letter became the living "bible" of the Freedom Movement.

During Dr. King's time in prison, the bail problem had been solved by Harry Belafonte, who had raised an extra 50,000 dollars.

Dr. King and Reverend Abernathy were released after eight days. Now was the time to organize for the big push. Martin Luther King appealed to the Negro students in the area, and they flocked to join the movement. Some of them were as young as six.

On Thursday, May 2, a thousand young Negroes marched on downtown Birmingham. Almost all of them were arrested. The next day another wave, even larger, marched to the battle field.

Faced with this open display of quiet force, Bull Connor lost his patience. He ordered his policemen to bring up high-powered water hoses. Streams of water knocked over the marchers and rolled them into the street. The police then moved in with clubs and dogs.

The next day Americans saw pictures of police dogs attacking the legs of Negro children. These pictures brought the anger of many Americans down on Birmingham's leaders. They also brought sympathy to the marchers and funds to the campaign.

On May 6 and 7, the marchers set forth again. Birmingham was on the edge of disaster. Business men called a meeting of white leaders to discuss peace. At first they were against all plans that were suggested, but when the meeting broke up for lunch they went outside to find that thousands of Negroes had again marched on the town. By this time the jails were so full that only a few could be arrested.

The business men were so impressed that they returned from lunch anxious to solve the problem.

After hours of discussion, these agreements were reached on May 10: (1) No segregation at lunch counters, rest rooms, fitting rooms, and drinking fountains; (2) hiring without regard to color; (3) help from city officials in releasing all jailed marchers; and (4) the forming of a committee made up of both whites and Negroes to discuss problems.

Resistance in Birmingham had crumbled before the greater force of non-violence. But peace did not come at once. The home of Dr. King's brother, the Reverend A. D. King, was bombed by the Ku Klux Klan the next night. A bomb was planted near the Gaston Motel where Dr. King and other leaders had stayed during the struggle. The bombs started going off about the same time the bars closed, and many local Negroes struck back. They threw stones and bottles at the police, turned cars over, and set fire to two apartment houses.

Dr. King was in Atlanta. He rushed back to Birmingham to try to calm the Negroes. After a few hours the trouble died down.

The Birmingham victory was capped by Bull Connor's removal from office. During the period of the demonstrations there had been a city election in which Connor had run for mayor. Connor did not win the election, but neither of the other two candidates got the necessary number of votes to win either. Another election was held and this time Connor lost. Meanwhile a new Commissioner of Public Safety had been elected, but Connor refused to give up this post. Instead, he started a suit which, if he had won, would have kept him in power for two more years.

A short time after the "Project C" victory, the Alabama Supreme Court ruled against Connor, and he was put out of office.

To Martin Luther King, one of the most important results of "Project C" was the full-scale entrance of the federal government into the field of human rights.

In a speech on June 11, President Kennedy said: "One hundred years of delay have passed since President Lincoln freed the slaves, yet their grandsons are not fully free. . . . Now the time has come for this nation to carry out its promise. The events in Birmingham and elsewhere have so increased the cries for equal rights that no city or state can fail to hear them."

A reply to the President's words was heard in Jackson, Mississippi, the next day. Medgar Evers, an NAACP field secretary, was murdered by white men.

A week later, President Kennedy presented Congress with a sweeping civil rights bill. In his message urging

Congress to pass it, he said: ". . . Justice requires us to assure the blessings of liberty for all Americans—not merely for reasons of economic efficiency, world diplomacy and domestic tranquility—but above all, because it is right."

CHAPTER 13

"I Have a Dream"

The Birmingham campaign had made millions of Americans very much aware of the crimes angry whites were capable of committing. Many Americans realized a new pride from the success of the Negro struggle, as the campaign moved on to other towns and cities.

Great steps had been taken toward freedom. Now one large, peaceful event was needed to show the public that the Freedom Movement was wide spread and here to stay. A. Philip Randolph again, as he had for years, urged a March on Washington. Martin Luther King and other leaders stood behind the idea. It was the 100th anniversary of the Emancipation Proclamation, and a march to the Lincoln Memorial was decided upon. The date was set for August 28, 1963.

It was the largest civil rights demonstration ever held and the largest crowd that had ever gathered in the nation's capital. Two hundred and fifty thousand Americans—at least one-fourth of them white—marched side by side in a show of human strength. They were of all ages, and they came from every state, class, profession and faith. White church organizations announced their support and sent many people.

All through the long, hot day the huge, peaceful army sang songs and listened to speeches from civil rights and religious leaders.

Dr. King was the last speaker. When he appeared, a spark of excitement ran through the crowd. At first, he read from a prepared speech.

"We cannot turn back," he said. "We can never be satisfied as long as a Negro in Mississippi cannot vote and a Negro in New York believes he has nothing for which to vote."

Then he reached into his heart and told the crowd. "I have a dream today. I have a dream that my four little children will one day live in a nation where they will not be judged by the color of their skin but by the content of their character.

"I have a dream," he repeated, his voice full of emotion, "that one day every valley shall be raised, every hill and mountain shall be made low, the rough places will be made plain, and the crooked places will be made straight, and the glory of the Lord shall be revealed, and all flesh shall see it together. . . .

"This is our hope. This is the faith with which I return to the South. . . . With this faith we will be able to work together, to pray together, to struggle together, to go to jail together, to stand up for freedom together, knowing that we will be free one day. . . .

"When we let freedom ring, when we let it ring from every village and every town, from every state and every city, we will be able to speed up that day when all of God's children, black men and white men, Jews and Gentiles, Protestants and Catholics, will be able to join hands and sing in the words of that old Negro song, 'Free at last! Free at last! Thank God Almighty, we are free at last!'"

At the end of his speech a wave of cheers rolled along the Potomac and swept on to the Washington Monument. Many in the crowd wept.

The speech was quoted throughout the country. President Kennedy met with the leaders of the march later in the day and told the press: "The nation can properly be proud of the demonstration that has occurred here today."

The March on Washington had made many Americans realize that civil rights are the responsibilities as well as the rights of every citizen. But not all agreed. That was shown once again on September 15.

It was less than three weeks since the March on Washington, which had been widely praised for its peaceful character. Peace did seem to have settled across the land that Sunday morning as millions of Americans, black and white, attended the churches of their choice.

The scene at the Sixteenth Street Baptist Church in Birmingham resembled that in thousands of other churches. Little boys and girls, dressed in their "Sunday best," trooped in to say their Sunday school verses and to be told Bible stories. Games and quarrels were set aside while they came together to hear the word of God.

During the Sunday school hour a car sped down Sixteenth Street. A few seconds later, as the car passed the church, a hand reached out of the window and tossed a bomb. The Sunday school room that had been so peaceful a moment before burst into flames. Four young Negro girls were killed instantly, and 14 other Negroes were injured. The men who did it were never brought to justice.

This crime angered white America. But instead of helping the Freedom Movement, it divided the ranks of

Negro leaders. Some wanted to start mass demonstrations again. Others wanted to return fire with fire.

The year 1963 had already been filled with acts of terror. Yet one more tragedy was still to come—the murder of President Kennedy in Dallas on November 22. Americans were struck with a grief they had not known since the death of President Lincoln a century before.

Martin Luther King wrote: "We were all involved in the death of John Kennedy. We tolerated hate; we tolerated violence in all walks of life; and tolerated the idea that a man's life was sacred only if we agreed with his views."

The new President, Lyndon B. Johnson, addressing Congress a few days later, said: "No speech could better honor President Kennedy's memory than the earliest possible passage of the civil rights bill for which he fought so long. . . . John Kennedy's death commands . . . that America must move forward."

America did begin to move forward. The nation struggled toward the new knowledge that human rights were for everyone and that hate and violence had no place in a free land. Violence has broken out across the country since that time, but the great events of 1963 made civil and human rights the concerns of every American. These rights were recognized as necessary. The nation would never be able to turn its back on them again.

Martin Luther King, Jr. came from the battlefield of

1963 with both scars and praise. *Time* magazine named him "Man of the Year," the first Negro to be chosen. The award is given to the man or woman who was most in the news of that year and left the deepest mark on history. No one could say that Martin Luther King was not a proper choice.

The magazine selected Dr. King "as a man—but also as representative of his people, for whom 1963 was perhaps the most important year in their history."

Time described Birmingham as the main battle ground of the "Negro Revolution" and said: "Martin Luther King, Jr., the leader of the Negroes in Birmingham, became to millions, black and white, in South and North, the sign of the revolution—and the Man of the Year."

In accepting the honor, Martin Luther King said that it was "not a personal honor, but an honor to the whole Freedom Movement."

CHAPTER 14

"We Shall Overcome"

It was time, Martin Luther King told a press conference, to start on a new kind of political action—getting Negroes to register to vote.

A few months later, Dr. King selected St. Augustine, Florida, for his peaceful protest campaign. There were reasons for this choice. St. Augustine, the oldest city in America, was celebrating its four-hundredth anniversary. A center of the slave trade in its early days, it had changed little in four centuries. In 1964 it was about 99 percent segregated.

The peaceful protest campaign opened at Easter and struggled through May and June. In addition to sit-ins and kneel-ins, Negro citizens marched at night through the old slave market.

In the Birmingham campaign, the marchers had been attacked by the police, but white residents had left them alone. In St. Augustine, the situation was reversed. The police did not interfere with the marchers, but neither did they attempt to stop white gangs who attacked them with clubs, chains, bricks and acid.

Martin Luther King appealed to the President, and at the same time staged a stand-in at a white restaurant. King, Reverend Abernathy and 14 others were arrested and jailed under Florida's "unwanted guest" law. Two days later, King was released on $900 bail.

What happened next formed a strange contrast. Martin Luther King went directly from the Florida jail to Yale University, where he was given an honorary degree for refusing to use violence. Ten thousand people rose to their feet and cheered him.

When the ceremony ended, he returned to the struggle in St. Augustine, where his latest honor meant nothing to the white mob. On the whole, the marchers in St. Augustine suffered more physical injuries than they had in any other protest campaign.

After two months of almost total "war," a peaceful agreement was reached with city officials. It was a hollow victory, however, as whites moved in quickly and forced business owners to restore segregation. The period of integration lasted exactly five days.

Then on July 2, the new Civil Rights Bill was passed by Congress. This was the strong bill President Kennedy had sent to Congress a few months before he was killed. It called for desegregation of public places and an end to bars against voting and jobs.

As a part of his new political activity, Martin Luther King spoke before both the Republican and Democratic conventions that summer and urged them to put civil rights planks in their platforms. To the Democrats he proposed a "Bill of Rights for the Disadvantaged." During the election campaign, Dr. King strongly favored President Johnson for his firm support of civil rights legislation and just as strongly opposed the Republican candidate, Barry Goldwater, for his veiled appeals to segregationists.

In September, Dr. King was invited by Willy Brandt, the mayor of West Berlin, to visit the divided city in Germany and take part in a service in memory of President Kennedy. He also went to the other side of the Berlin Wall to preach a sermon at one of the city's oldest churches.

Dr. King and Reverend Abernathy, who was traveling

with him, then flew to Rome, where they had a private talk with Pope Paul VI. The Pope proved to be fully informed about the Negro struggle in America and expressed his sympathy. He presented Dr. King with a medal struck in honor of the Second Vatican Council and asked him for copies of his two latest books.

It was a year of high honors, but the greatest was yet to come. On October 15, it was announced in the world press that Martin Luther King had won the Nobel Peace Prize, which is given to the person who has done most to help make all men brothers.

He was the third Negro and the youngest person to receive the award since it was established in 1895 by Alfred Nobel, the Swedish inventor of dynamite. The prize carried with it $56,400. Dr. King promised that "every penny" of the money would go toward continuing the civil rights movement.

On December 10, 1964, Martin Luther King, Jr. made his speech accepting the award before the largest crowd ever assembled for the Nobel Peace Prize ceremonies in Oslo, Norway.

"I accept the Nobel Prize for Peace at a moment when twenty-two million Negroes of the United States of America are engaged in a creative battle to end the long night of racial injustice. I accept this award in behalf of a civil rights movement which is moving with determination and a majestic scorn for risk and danger to establish a reign of freedom and a rule of justice. I am mindful that only yesterday in Birmingham, Alabama, our children, crying out for brotherhood, were answered with fire hoses, snarling dogs, and even death. I am mindful that only yesterday in Philadelphia, Mississippi, young people seeking to secure the right to vote were brutalized and murdered. And only yesterday, more than forty houses of worship in the State of Mississippi alone were bombed or burned because they offered a sanctuary to those who would not accept segregation. I am mindful that debilitating and grinding poverty afflicts my people and chains them to the lowest rung of the economic ladder.

"The tortuous road which has led from Montgomery, Alabama, to Oslo bears witness of this truth. This is a road which millions of Negroes are traveling to find a new sense of dignity. This same road has opened for all Americans a new era of progress and hope. It has led to a new Civil Rights Bill, and it will, I am convinced, be widened and lengthened into a super highway of justice as Negro and white men in increasing numbers create alliances to overcome their common problem.

". . . I believe that unarmed truth and unconditional love will have the final word in reality. This is why right temporarily defeated is stronger than evil triumphant. I believe that even amid today's . . . whining bullets, there is still hope for a brighter tomorrow. I believe that wounded justice, lying prostrate on the blood-flowing streets of our nations, can be lifted from this dust of shame to reign supreme among the children of men. I have the audacity to believe that peoples everywhere can have three meals a day for their bodies, education and culture for their minds, and dignity, equality, and freedom for their spirits. I believe that what self-centered men have torn down other-centered men can build up. I still believe that one day mankind will bow before the altars of God and be crowned triumphant over war and bloodshed, and non-violent redemptive good will proclaimed the rule of the land. 'And the lion and the lamb shall lie down together and every man shall sit under his own vine and fig tree and none shall be afraid.' I still believe that we *shall* overcome!

". . . I accept this award . . . in trust for its true owners—all those to whom beauty is truth and truth beauty—and in whose eyes the beauty of genuine brotherhood and peace is more precious than diamonds or silver or gold."

CHAPTER 15

From Selma to Montgomery

Only a month after Martin Luther King returned from the Nobel Peace Prize ceremonies in Oslo, he began the Selma, Alabama, campaign to register Negroes to vote.

Dr. King realized, as did many other Americans, that in spite of the strong provisions in the Civil Rights Act of 1964, millions of Negroes in the South were being denied the right to vote.

He wanted to bring this fact before the public and make the President and Congress aware that more laws were needed. Selma was a perfect example. Only two percent of its Negro population of voting age had even been allowed to register to vote.

King had said earlier, "Give us the vote and we will no longer plead." Now he wrote an article that appeared in *The New York Times*, saying that the vote could be used to sweep out of office public officials who denied Negroes their rights to good homes, public safety, jobs, and education.

"We are going to bring a voting bill into being in the streets of Selma," he said, as the campaign began. It was January 1965.

Selma was soon filled with Negro marchers. Their goal was the county court house where they hoped to get the people out to register. A few registered, but most were arrested or turned away. The jails slowly filled up. Those who were sent away marched again the following day.

Martin Luther King led the march on February 1 and was also arrested. He was charged with "parading without a permit." Jailed with him were about 500 school children and 263 older people.

With the news of the arrest of the Nobel Peace Prize winner, world-wide attention turned toward Selma. King could have put up bond and been released at once, but he chose to remain in jail to put the pressure on county officials.

In "A Letter from a Selma, Alabama Jail," he wrote: "When the King of Norway participated in awarding the Nobel Peace Prize to me, he surely did not think that in less than 60 days I would be in jail. . . . Why are we in jail? . . . This is Selma, Alabama. There are more Negroes in jail with me than there are on the voting rolls."

After he was released on February 5, huge demonstrations began. They continued for the next seven weeks. More than 2,000 men, women, and children were arrested. Even so, there was little action from the general public. The Selma campaign slowed down. It might have ended in defeat if whites had not committed an act of violence.

On February 18, another civil rights march took place in Marion, Alabama, 30 miles from Selma. It had been a peaceful demonstration until Alabama state police and other whites moved in to attack. Fighting broke out and one of the Negro marchers, 26-year-old Jimmie Lee Jackson, was shot in the stomach. He accused a state policeman of firing the bullet. Eight days later he died.

Jackson's funeral was held on March 3. It was attended by 4,000 Negro mourners. In his funeral address, Martin Luther King said that Jimmie Lee Jackson's death meant that Negroes had to work harder and harder to make the American dream a reality. Jimmie Lee Jackson was dead, but the Selma campaign was born again.

However, victory still seemed remote. Dr. King felt that a larger mass action was needed. He wanted to make the Alabama leaders aware that Jackson's death would not stop the Selma campaign. Also, he felt that a show of non-violence would bring the voting issue more sharply before the American public.

He announced a mass march from Selma to Montgomery, the state capital, and set March 7 as the starting date. "But I can't promise you that it won't get you beaten," he warned his audience.

When news of the march reached Alabama Governor George Wallace, he said he would not allow it. But that did not stop the marchers from beginning their 54-mile procession. King was in Atlanta that day, and the march out of Selma was led by John Lewis of SNCC and by an assistant to King, Hosea Williams. About 550 Negroes and a few whites walked peacefully through Selma and crossed the Edmund Pettus Bridge.

A solid block of state police was waiting for them on the other side of the bridge, armed with pistols, clubs, and tear gas. The sheriff, with more than a hundred armed men, some of them on horseback, backed up the state police.

As the marchers approached, a police officer ordered them to stop. They stopped. They were then ordered to break up within two minutes. When the marchers did not respond the officer boomed out: "State police, advance!"

Swinging their clubs, the state police descended on the marchers. The sheriff's men advanced at the same time. The Negro marchers were stung by the tips of bull whips and knocked down under horses' hoofs. A crowd of whites stood a safe distance from the action and howled their approval.

Having protected themselves with masks, the state police fired on the demonstrators with tear gas. When they attemped to flee the gas attacks, the sheriff's men chased them with clubs and bull whips. The marchers gained the safety of a nearby church. There, many were treated for wounds. Seventeen had to be taken to the hospital with broken limbs and other injuries.

Pictures of the attack appeared the next day in newspapers and on TV. The American people, who had not appeared to be very interested during the first weeks of the campaign, were now aroused. People came from all over the country to join the marchers, among them several hundred white ministers.

On Monday, Martin Luther King returned from Atlanta with the intention of leading another march. Meanwhile, his lawyers had asked for a federal court order that would forbid state police from stopping or attacking the marchers.

The march was scheduled for Tuesday. The federal

judge announced that he would not hear the case before Thursday. King preferred to wait for the decision, which he was sure would be favorable, but the marchers were anxious to leave on Tuesday, even without a guarantee of protection.

Under great pressure from both sides, Martin Luther King came to an agreement with the federal mediators sent in by President Johnson. He would lead the band of marchers, now swelled to 1,500 persons, to the bridge where they were attacked before; he would then lead them back to Selma again.

This much of the Selma-to-Montgomery march took place on Tuesday. But when the leaders of other civil rights groups learned that the march had been cut short through a private agreement with the government, they were so angry that they threatened to withdraw their support from the whole campaign.

Again the "Battle of Selma" seemed about to be lost. Again the cause was advanced by attacks from a white mob. Three white ministers were beaten, and one of the three, Reverend James Reeb of Boston, died as a result.

The death of Jimmie Lee Jackson had not had much effect outside the Negro community, but the death of Reverend Reeb sparked demonstrations all through the country. Demands for federal help in Alabama poured into the White House. President Johnson publicly condemned the violence in Selma. He also promised to send

Congress a new bill that would strike down all methods used to deny people the right to vote.

It now appeared that the "Battle of Selma" was won—but at the cost of two lives and much suffering.

President Johnson kept his promise. On March 15, he made a TV appearance before Congress. "I speak tonight for the dignity of man," the President said. "At times history and fate meet at a single time in a single place to shape a turning point in man's search for freedom.

"So it was at Lexington and Concord. So it was a century ago at Appomattox. So it was last week in Selma, Alabama. . . ."

He went on to speak of the "fact . . . that in many places in this country men and women are kept from voting simply because they are Negroes.

"Their cause must be our cause too," he continued. "Because it's not just Negroes, but really it's all of us who must overcome . . . injustice.

"And we shall overcome."

President Johnson did send his voting rights bill to Congress. Congress passed the bill, and the President signed it into law on August 6, 1965.

Two days after the President's speech, a federal judge granted permission for the march from Selma to Montgomery. He also ordered the state police not to interfere with the marchers but to give them protection if gangs of whites attacked.

At 1 P.M., Sunday, March 21, 3,200 members of the Freedom Movement sang "We Shall Overcome" one last time before beginning the march to Montgomery. The marchers were led by Martin and Coretta King, United Nations official, Dr. Ralph Bunche, and many other well-known Negro and white leaders. The marchers had come from all over the country. Resembling the quarter million people at the March on Washington in 1963, they came from every class, age, and profession. There were workers and labor leaders, students and professors and ministers.

The actor Gary Merrill was one of those who joined the marchers. When asked why, he replied: "Because I was too young for Lexington and Concord."

This march was far different from the first march to Montgomery, which had ended in tragedy. This time the marchers had the protection of the United States Government. The President had put the Alabama National Guard under federal orders and sent in 4,000 U. S. Army troops.

The federal court order allowed only 300 to march the entire 54 miles, so the remaining 2,900 returned to Selma that evening.

The Kings had to leave the march on Tuesday, but they returned on Wednesday afternoon. That night the marchers camped out near Montgomery, where they were joined by thousands of people who had come to walk the final three and a half miles.

The last slow lap was led by the 300 tired men and women who had walked the entire distance from Selma. King, Bunche, A. Philip Randolph, and other leaders came next. Following them were tens of thousands of ordinary American citizens. Black and white, they, too, displayed their belief in civil rights for all.

The marchers halted before the state capitol, the beautiful building that had once been headquarters of the Confederacy. A bill for Negro rights in Alabama had been drawn up, which the leaders wanted to present to Governor Wallace in person. The Governor peered out at the huge crowd and sent a message that he would not see them, but this no longer mattered so much.

The Selma campaign, at first intended to get more Negroes to register to vote, had ended in a national victory. For Martin Luther King, Jr., the return to Montgomery was one of triumph. The Dexter Avenue Baptist Church, where he had begun his career as a minister ten years before, could still be seen from the capitol steps. It was here that he had first put into practice his policy of non-violence. It was the Negroes of Montgomery who had said "No" to being second-class citizens, and who had given Negroes everywhere a new pride and hope.

When he spoke now before the marchers who filled

the square, Dr. King reminded them of the major strides that had been made in the last ten years. "We are on the move now," he said. "Yes, we are on the move. . . .

"Let us therefore continue our triumph. . . . Let us march on segregated schools. . . . Let us march on poverty. . . . Let us march on the ballot boxes. . . ."

He went on to remind the crowd that these marches must be made in the spirit of non-violence. "Our aim must never be to defeat . . . the white man but to win his friendship and understanding. We must come to see that the end we seek is a society at peace with itself, a society that can live with its conscience. That will be a day not of the white man, not of the black man. That will be the day of man as man."

CHAPTER 16

"Mine Eyes Have Seen the Glory"

Much had been accomplished since the time, almost ten years earlier, when the Montgomery bus boycott had begun. Now the question facing Martin Luther King was: *Where do we go from here?*

In a world torn apart by war, there was no simple answer. Martin Luther King still had the greatest following, both black and white, of any person in the civil rights movement. But the movement itself was being split up into several different groups, each with its own leader.

Some of these new leaders were impatient with Dr. King's policy of non-violence and were calling for "black power."

By December 1966, Martin Luther King had found his answer. He began by accusing the Government of the United States of placing the Vietnam war ahead of better houses, education, and job opportunities at home.

His stand against the war in Vietnam stirred up a storm of protest. Many Americans, among them other Negro leaders, spoke against him. Over night, thousands who had admired him declared that he was in the wrong.

To his congregation at the Ebenezer Baptist Church in Atlanta, he said that those who were against him now had never really understood him in the first place.

"As a minister of God," he said, "and as a winner of the Nobel Peace Prize, I have the mission to work harder for peace and I plan to do just that."

As the number of people opposing him grew, others came to his defense. James P. Brown, writing in *The Providence Journal*, said:

". . . Dr. King is not just another Negro fighting for his rights. He is a minister of God, . . . of the Prince of Peace and of Gandhi. As a man of conscience, he is compelled to speak out against the wrong of the Vietnam war. . . ."

Other individuals and groups, notably the National Council of Churches, later came forward to defend him. Dr. King welcomed this support and at the same time insisted that his opposition to "our policy in Vietnam" was a personal moral stand.

In April 1967, he became co-chairman of Clergy and Laymen Concerned About Vietnam, a national peace organization. Later that month he started a grass-roots peace movement. This was followed by a call for 10,000 people to work in 500 communities all through the summer.

His work for peace led to a suggestion that he run for President of the United States.

He refused to consider becoming a candidate, saying, "I think of my role as one which operates outside . . . politics."

Some people accused Dr. King of losing interest in the struggle for civil rights. He replied that he was as much involved in civil rights as ever. He continued to lead drives for voter registration and for open housing.

Martin Luther King had chosen to go his own way, to help where he thought his help would do the most good. When whole blocks in sections of Newark and Detroit went up in flames in the "long, hot summer" of 1967, Dr. King supported the President's decision to send federal troops in to stop the riots, although he attacked the causes of the troubles.

"We had a long, cold winter when little was done about the conditions that create riots," he said. He called riots "the language of the unheard" and declared, "Revolts come from revolting conditions." Once again, he spoke out against the Administration for putting the Vietnam war ahead of poverty programs. He recommended a huge government program to end slums and to provide more jobs for Negroes.

Throughout the remainder of 1967, Dr. King continued to protest against the war. In one of his major statements he said: "A nation that continues . . . to spend more money on military defense than on programs of social uplift is approaching spiritual death."

Dr. King planned a "poor people's march" on Washington for the spring of 1968, hoping to further dramatize the need for an end to slum conditions.

While he was still forming these plans, Dr. King went to Memphis, Tennessee, in April to lead a non-violent march in support of local garbage workers—most of them Negroes—who were striking for better pay and working conditions.

On the evening of April 4, while he was leaning over the balcony of his motel to chat with friends, Dr. Martin Luther King was shot. He died immediately.

Dr. King had known for a long time that his life was in danger, but he had refused to abandon his work. Only 24 hours before he was murdered he said:

"Like anybody, I would like to live a long life. . . . But I'm not concerned about that now. I just want to do God's will.

"And he's allowed me to go up to the mountain. And I've looked over, and I've seen the promised land.

"I may not get there with you, but I want you to know tonight that we as a people will get to the promised land.

"So I'm happy tonight. I'm not worried about anything. I'm not fearing any man. Mine eyes have seen the glory of the coming of the Lord."

Martin Luther King's funeral was held at the Ebenezer Baptist Church in Atlanta on April 9, 1968. After the service, his casket was put on a farm wagon drawn by two mules and taken to Morehouse College, where a service in his memory was held. More than 150,000 mourners walked behind the wagon. It was the largest number of people ever to attend a private funeral in the United States.

Martin Luther King was buried in South View cemetery near his grandparents. Carved on his gravestone are the words from an old slave song:

> Free at last,
> Free at last,
> Thank God Almighty, I'm free at last.